Asbury Theological Seminary

90th Anniversary

Publications

Henry Clay Morrison
"Crusader Saint"
by Percival A. Wesche

A Short History of Asbury Theological Seminary
by Howard Fenimore Shipps

The Distinctive Emphases of Asbury Theological Seminary
by Harold B. Kuhn

Theological Foundations
Fiftieth Anniversary Scholarly Essays

All Things Are Ours...
Photographic Record of Asbury's Fiftieth Year

Asbury Theological Seminary

90th Anniversary

Publications

Audio Recordings from the 50th Anniversary Celebration
and Special Lecture Series
March 11-15, 1974

50th Anniversary Banquet Speeches
*by Franklin D. Morrison, Frank Bateman Stanger, and
J. C. McPheeters*

**"Salvation Today," "Ingredients of the Gospel,"
"The Mind of Christ," and "Keep the Hope of Heaven"**
by Bishop Roy C. Nichols

"Whither Wesleyan Theology?" in four parts
by Dr. Albert C. Outler

"Whiter Christology?" in four parts
by Dr. C.F.D. Moule

"Whither Mission?" in four parts
by Bishop Stephen Neill

The 90th Anniversary Publications are available in digital form for free through First Fruits Press. They can be found by visiting First Fruits' Website, under the Heritage Collection: place.asburyseminary.edu/firstfruits

A Short History

of

Asbury Theological Seminary

Howard Fenimore Shipps

First Fruits Press
Wilmore, Kentucky
c2012

ISBN: 9781621710455

A Short History of Asbury Theological Seminary by Howard Fenimore Shipps.
First Fruits Press, © 2013 | Seminary Press, ©1963

Digital version at http://place.asburyseminary.edu/firstfruitsheritagematerial/22

For all other uses, contact:

First Fruits Press
B.L. Fisher Library
Asbury Theological Seminary
204 N. Lexington Ave.
Wilmore, KY 40390
http://place.asburyseminary.edu/firstfruits

Shipps, Howard Fenimore, 1903-
    A short history of Asbury Theological Seminary / Howard Fenimore Shipps.
    vi, 114 p. ; 21 cm.
    2nd ed. / revised by Faith E. Parry and Robert Danielson
    Wilmore, Ky. : First Fruits Press, c2013.
    Originally published: Wilmore, Ky. : Seminary Press, c1963.
    Asbury Theological Seminary 90th Anniversary Publications ; no. 2
    ISBN: 9781621710455 (pbk.)
    1. Asbury Theological Seminary – History. 2. Theological seminaries – Kentucky –
    Wilmore – History. I. Title. II. Series.
    BV4070.A5756 S5 2013   378.992

Cover design by Kelli Dierdorf

asburyseminary.edu
800.2ASBURY
204 North Lexington Avenue
Wilmore, Kentucky 40390

First Fruits
THE ACADEMIC OPEN PRESS OF ASBURY SEMINARY

A Short History

of

Asbury Theological

Seminary

Howard Fenimore Shipps

Professor Church History

Seminary Press
Wilmore, Kentucky
c1963

Preface

No observance of the anniversary of the founding of a graduate school of theology would be complete without significant publications. The Fortieth Anniversary Committee is pleased to present to the friends of Asbury Theological Seminary this significant trilogy of books: *Henry Clay Morrison Crusader Saint, The History of Asbury Theological Seminary,* and *The Distinctive Emphases of Asbury Theological Seminary.*

We congratulate the members of the Fortieth Anniversary Editorial Committee—Dr. Harold B. Kuhn, chairman, Dr. J. Harold Greenlee, and Dr. George A. Turner—for their excellent work, and we commend to you the careful reading of these three significant Fortieth Anniversary volumes.

Frank Bateman Stanger
President of the Seminary and
General Chairman of the Fortieth
Anniversary Committee

Table of Contents

Introduction

It has been suggested that the story of Asbury Theological Seminary be told within the compass of this little volume numbering less than one hundred pages. What an assignment! However the attempt is being made with the hope that the purpose of such an assignment may at least in some measure be fulfilled. The limitations upon such an attempt are numerous. We trust that they will be understood and appreciated by the reader.

The actual time of the founding of the Seminary was 1923, and the major emphasis will be put upon the events and developments that have taken place during the four decades from that year to the present. However, there is a meaningful continuity between the spirit and life of this theological institution and the historic Christian community even from apostolic times. Especially will this continuity be observed in the relationship that Asbury has maintained with Methodism.

Heretofore there have been no published works dealing exclusively with the history either of Asbury College or of the Seminary. Three unpublished works, however, have been produced, one on the history of the College and two on the history of the Seminary. Each of these was written as a master's thesis. In 1926 Earl Stanley McKee dealt with the early history of Asbury in a thesis entitled, *The Early History of Asbury College*, 1890-1910. This is available at the library of the University of

Kentucky. Twenty-three years later, in 1949, Robert Owen Fraley wrote a master's thesis entitled, *A Complete History of Asbury Theological Seminary*. A copy of this may be found in the Asbury Seminary library. Only two years after the work of Mr. Fraley, Paul Frederick Abel produced a master's thesis, which he submitted in partial fulfillment of the requirements for the degree of Master of Arts in Columbia University. The title of this thesis is *An Historical Study of The Origin and Development of Asbury Theological Seminary*, and it is available both at the library of Columbia University and at the Asbury Seminary library. Permission from the latter two writers, Fraley and Abel, for the free use of materials included in their theses has been obtained by the committee on publication of The Fortieth Anniversary of Asbury Theological Seminary. Specific reference in the use of such materials will therefore usually be omitted. The author of this history wishes to acknowledge his debt not only to these, but also to any others whose writings have furnished significant information in this popular telling of the story of Asbury Theological Seminary. It will be understood by the reader that the limitation of space for this anniversary volume will make it impossible to include references or footnotes. The works referred to above will provide such references for the scholar who may desire to pursue a more thorough study.

Chapter 1
Apostolic Origins

The knowledge of one's ancestry is usually of considerable interest to the normal person. A goodly and especially a godly heritage is an endowment of boundless worth. It is likewise right that an institution as well as an individual should be much interested in the ancestry and the tradition, which has made a major contribution to its life.

The attempt to lay claim to apostolic beginnings by numerous reform institutions has become so general that the very attitude may now be looked upon as trite or commonplace. But the ultimate demonstration of such claim must rest upon the ability to perform. As some one has observed, the evidence of divine ability is not determined so much by apostolic succession as by apostolic success.

The church through the centuries has been influenced, and in a very real sense, controlled, by reform and puritan movements. The puritan reform across the years has often been extreme and occasionally radical in its partially misguided attempt to purify the church. And yet upon many occasions such movements have been the saviors of the church. From the earliest times in the life of the Christian community the church has been involved with this movement, usually arising from within its own body. The attempt of such a movement has been

1

to regulate, adjust, reform, and always ultimately to purify and thus strengthen. The earliest well-organized attempt to accomplish these objectives was by the Montanists of the second century. The occasion of the rise of this reform was threefold:

1) The church of the second century had in large measure lost the early hope of the imminent return of Christ.
2) The universal presence and ministry of the Holy Spirit in the lives of all Christians, which was so characteristic of the apostolic churches, had definitely declined.
3) The church of the second century had already begun to show marked signs of worldliness. Montanism at its best was an attempt to correct all these conditions within the church. Of course it also held notions that were extreme and radical, but seldom has any reform movement been unmixed with some measure of error. Such purifying attempts have appeared within the church across the centuries, Donatism, the spirituals among the Franciscans, Anabaptism, Puritanism, Pietism, and others. They have urgently issued their protest against the contemporary evils, which have appeared as a serious threat to the life and influence of the church. Usually their own life and example have been a wholesome force against the various evils of the church.

Such purifying reactions within the church have maintained certain characteristics in common. Very briefly they may be stated as follows:

1) Concern about the law of spiritual gravitation within the Christian community—the appearance of second and third generation Christians with little evidence of divine life within.
2) Reaction against the *status quo* of the church.
3) Desire for apostolic simplicity and purity.
4) Often a spirit of censoriousness and destructive criticism.

Methodism in its earliest manifestation was a movement of the Spirit. It takes its place in the long line of enterprises toward reform. It was as the Protestant Reformation had been, not something new, but rather a rediscovery of something that had been lost in the accumulation of secondary and external things during the generations of spiritual decline. The doctrine of justification by faith was not new to the church, but it had been so obscured by the multiplication of ecclesiastical and legalistic elements of religion during the middle ages, that it had to be rediscovered by Luther in the sixteenth century. So it was with Methodism in the eighteenth century. Its great central doctrines, such as the witness of the Spirit, assurance, and Christian holiness, were not new, but they had been generally lost to the Christian community of Wesley's day. Methodism therefore, like Protestantism, is a rediscovery of certain lost truths.

Abel Stevens in his analysis of Methodism affirms "it is a revival church in its spirit, a missionary church in its organization, and a resuscitation of the spiritual life and practical aims of primitive Christianity." As a positive and aggressive effort toward reform, Methodism stood in contrast to the *status quo* of Anglicanism. Even Isaac Taylor admits that when Wesley appeared the Anglican church was "an ecclesiastical system under which the people of England had lapsed into heathenism, or a state hardly to be distinguished from it," and that Methodism "preserved from extinction and reanimated the languishing nonconformity of the last century, which, just at the time of the Methodist revival, was rapidly in course to be found nowhere but in books."

In general then it may be observed that Methodism became a purifying reform movement for eighteenth century England and ultimately for much of the world. As Montanism was to the Christian community of the second century; as Protestantism was to the Christianity of the middle ages; as German Pietism was to the Lutheran church of the seventeenth century, so Methodism became to Anglicanism of the eighteenth. As a part of an apostolic force in modern times it was not reactionary, and yet it was positively puritan and constructively revolutionary. Cyril Richardson, in his volume, *The Church Through the Centuries* (page 203) says:

> In its origins Methodism was a revolt against the general spirit of the Enlightenment in eighteenth-century England. It stressed vital, personal religion in contrast to the cold rationalism of that epoch. It preached Christianity as a living experience and not as a moral code or an obsolete dogma. It had fever and conviction in an age that looked askance at all forms of enthusiasm and emotionalism. As a movement born within the Church of England it sought to revitalize ancient forms and traditions, and to make Christianity a vital way of life to nominal members of the church.

The evidences of such apostolic origins were as clearly seen in the beginnings of Methodism in America as they had been in the mother country. The spiritual enthusiasm and religious zeal, the outpourings of the Spirit from the presence of the Lord, and the mighty movements of genuine revival were characteristic of the American Methodist scene even before the formal organization of this church in 1784. The eighteenth century among the colonies was one of frequently repeated revival. Beginning with the tenants of the early twenties and continuing through the middle years of the century with the revival under the human direction of Whitefield, there had been almost a continuous religious stirring within the American society. This great awakening was to be continued and advanced by the leadership, which Methodism assumed just prior to the eve of the Revolution, and followed through most of the first half of the nineteenth century. It was during these decades that Methodism, while majoring on revival and apostolic simplicity, was making its great advances in numerical strength by keeping pace with the rapid increase in population, and also in developing its organizational structure.

In his volume, *Statistical History of the First Century of American Methodism*, C. C. Goss points out that from 1790 to 1865 the increase in Methodist membership far exceeded the increase in population. During this period the population in the United States advanced from 3,929,827 to 37,126,637, which represents an average increase for each decade of 35.8%. On the other hand American Methodism during the same period of time advanced from 57,631 to 929,259, which represents an average increase for each decade of 56.85%. The author in proposing to explain this remarkable success of Methodism suggests that the following characteristics were largely responsible:

1) The character of its preaching.
2) Self-sacrificing spirit of its ministry.
3) System of free churches.
4) Its frequent revivals.
5) Its lay activities.
6) Its missionary spirit.
7) Its positive Christian experience.
8) The doctrine of sanctification.

American Methodism, as it launched into the second century of its course, became increasingly aware that the law of spiritual gravitation was operating in its life, as it may be observed to operate in the life of any Christian community. Though it had achieved very large success and had risen to the place of greatest influence of any denomination within the States, yet there were also forces of deterioration at work. William Warren Sweet in his volume *Methodism in American History* (page 335), points out the evidences of this decline. He speaks of the years 1880-1900 as the gilded age and observes that in this period of transition the Methodist church was shifting from a "living organism" to a "mere mechanism." Emphasis upon organization and externalism had exceeded the emphasis upon personal Christian experience and spiritual growth. Sweet lists other symptoms of the serious decline in Methodism as follows:

1) The rise of the trustee and the decline of the leader and the steward.
2) The drying up of the local ministry.
3) The widespread and increasing laxity of discipline.
4) The toning down of the visible lines between the church and the world.
5) The uneasy doubt concerning positive conversion.
6) The loss of the grip on the masses, especially in the "best appointments."
7) The growth of professional evangelism.

And yet while these signs of peril were appearing, it must be remembered that there were also signs of maturing spiritual life and increasing power and Christian influence among the people called Methodists. Abel Stevens in his volume, *The Centenary of American Methodism* (page 105), affirms,

The church (Methodist) retained vividly the consciousness and spirit of its original mission as a revival of apostolic religion. Its ministry was remarkable for its unction and preached with demonstration and with power; its social and public worship was characterized by animation and energy; it was continually promoting revivals and reformations, extending them, not only over conferences or single states, but sometimes simultaneously over much of the nation. Therefore was its growth rapid beyond parallel.

This one sees that at the beginning of the second century of American Methodism the movement is aware of the presence of similar forces which have characterized the Christian community throughout all its lifetime. Increased emphasis upon material things usually diminishes the value placed upon the unseen and spiritual. Experiential religion and vital faith are often supplanted by the more legalistic aspects of religion. Personalized religion becomes institutionalized. All these indicated the urgent need for effective revival.

It was in the early years of this second century of Methodism in America that the Rev. John Wesley Hughes began to assume a place of leadership in revivalistic Methodism. He was a native of Kentucky, whose forbearers had dwelt in this state for three generations and who had earlier migrated from Virginia. Hughes was rightfully proud of his honest, industrious, middle-class ancestors whose sense of justice and righteousness contributed so much to the building of his own character. His call to preach, from the rural rustic life in which he participated as a boy in Owenton County, was clear and demanding. Whatever this lad did was always with great enthusiasm, and his response to God's call was no less so than any other activity of his life.

He entered the ministry with a total commitment of all his native powers touched by the redeeming riches of divine grace. He took advantage of the best educational opportunities, which were at his disposal. In addition to pursuing faithfully the course of theological training prescribed by The Methodist Conference, he attended the Kentucky Wesleyan College and Vanderbilt University. During the early years of his ministry in Kentucky he served the Lord and His church with remarkable success as pastor and evangelist. He freely shared his good ministerial gifts with many of his brethren, and under his leadership frequent revivals of religion came to pass not only within his own parish, but also throughout many communities of this state.

After twelve years as a pastor and one as an evangelist, Dr. Hughes felt a clear call to establish a college. Though he felt himself very much unprepared for this work, the urgent call of God persisted. He says in his *Autobiography* (page 99): "I hoped and prayed that I had misinterpreted the summons and that I might continue the work so dear to my heart (pastor and evangelist) –and in which I had had a good measure of success." The vision of the need for such Christian education seems to be used by God as an instrument to increase the urgency of the call. Hughes said again:

> I had seen and felt the need for years of a real salvation school where religious young men and women could hold their salvation; and where unsaved and unsanctified students would not only be encouraged, but urged to get saved and sanctified and prepared educationally for their life's work. ...I believed then, as I do now, that a rounded and complete education involved a genuine Christian experience. To educate the body to the neglect of the mind and the soul makes a man beastly. To educate the mind to the neglect of

the body and soul leads to dead intellectualism. To educate the soul to the neglect of mind and body results in fanaticism. I also believed then, as I do now, that a real Christian school would put the Bible in the curriculum, teaching the history, doctrine and experience of our holy Christianity daily, stressing the teaching of Jesus.

But who would God have to establish such an institution? Hughes saw the need and felt the call; but he also believed himself to be very poorly prepared for such a task. This call, of all that had come to him from God, involved the greatest struggle. Finally after days and nights of agonizing prayer he was captured by God for this work.

The school was founded by Hughes in September 1890, with eleven students and three teachers, and was originally known as The Kentucky Holiness College. This name was to be continued for only one year, when the founder affirmed that the Lord gave him the name as he waited before Him in prayer. It was to be Asbury College. Out of the reading of McTyeire's *History of Methodism,* Hughes suggests a very meaningful relation with Bethel Academy, which was established by Francis Asbury in 1790, just a century before Asbury College. Bethel was located only three and a half miles from Wilmore above the cliffs of the Kentucky River a little northeast of High Bridge. This was the second Methodist school in America, and undoubtedly has its truest line of descent through Asbury College and Asbury Theological Seminary. Continued Hughes:

> I felt that this was a providential coincidence, for all who know the history and character of Bishop Asbury, know that he contended earnestly, in common with Mr. Wesley and their coadjutors, for the faith, which was once delivered to the saints! This is, free salvation to all

men and full salvation from all sin, the secret of Asbury College's origin and success.

It seems quite clear in the light of the foregoing developments that the environment in which Asbury Theological Seminary was conceived was a movement striving for a purifying reform within Christianity in general and for the safeguarding of the original spirit and doctrinal foundations upon which Methodism had been established. The purpose of the founding of Asbury College was to unite in a proper and effective relation the normal development of mind, heart, and body. It was intended that this purpose should be realized in the lives of young people during the years in which they were pursuing a regular liberal arts course. The emphasis upon a specialized theological training appeared upon several occasions during the progress and expansion of the college. However, it was not until 1923 that the Seminary was established as a regular professional theological institution.

Chapter 2
Conceived and Dedicated

As has been indicated in the previous chapter, Asbury College was not primarily a theological institution. Its major concern was a vital, relevant Christian education at the college level. It must not be overlooked, however, that a real concern for theological education has been an important responsibility, which the College has assumed throughout its lifetime. As early as 1895, only five years after it's founding, the building program of Asbury included the Minister's Hall. This was a two-story frame building with sixteen dormitory rooms and two halls, which was to be used exclusively by young men preparing for the ministry. A year preceding the erection of this building a theological course had been added to the curriculum. Special emphasis was placed upon the Classics, English, Methodist Theology and the Discipline.

During the entire administration of President Hughes from 1890 to 1904, the fundamental and practical aspects of theological training were constantly emphasized. This was the natural result of at least two factors. First, Hughes himself was a practical and dynamic theologian and a sound philosopher, and therefore deeply concerned that the church should have the most thoroughly and effectively trained ministry. Second, the college was maintained under strict Christian influences and supported by many of the most devoted Christian homes within Methodism and other evangelical groups. Such homes usually provide a very congenial atmosphere in which the call of God to Christian service is apt to be heard more clearly.

It is of considerable interest to note, however, that the immediate successor of President Hughes sought to inaugurate the most ambitious and professional theological curriculum that had ever been imagined among the leaders of Asbury. The Reverend Francis F. Fitch of Marshall, Texas, in 1905, became the second president of Asbury College. Increased interest in theological studies during the Hughes administration was manifest by the enrollment of forty-eight ministerial students in the catalogue of 1904. Perhaps it was this enlarging body of prospective ministers that led President-Elect Fitch to suggest the academic foundation upon which he hoped soon to establish a fully accredited theological seminary. According to this plan, the fifth academic department of Asbury College was to be a School of Theology. The courses offered in this curriculum were to lead to the granting of three degrees, namely, Bachelor of Divinity, Doctor of Philosophy, and Doctor of Sacred Theology. The candidates who sought the attainment of these degrees were confronted with very formidable requirements. The mastering of the Hebrew and Greek languages in which the Scriptures were originally recorded, and of Latin, were basic requirements for all theological pursuits. In addition to these were prescribed advanced studies in Theology, History, Philosophy, English, Logic, Science, and Mathematics. The most stringent exactions seem to have been placed upon those in pursuit of the S. T. D. degree. These candidates must have completed four years of college with at least an average of 80 percent. They must also have completed the three-year graduate theological course in which they have maintained honor standing. In the practical area the students must have rendered to the church ten years of significant service as a kind of confirmation of the validity of their academic training. The final phase of the requirement for this advanced degree was a three-year's course of graduate study, and the preparation and publication of an acceptable thesis.

Such was the dream of President Fitch. Though it never came to actual fulfillment, it is most significant that the anticipation of this quality of theological achievement had its place in the minds of Asbury's leaders at so early a date. Further, it is of practical importance that throughout the forty years of Asbury Theological Seminary's life, many of the elements of the Fitch plan have been incorporated into the life of the institution. This plan at the time of its origin was surely a high ideal, and for a number of reasons was impossible of achievement at that time. But through the years it has been increasingly fulfilled; and undoubtedly the future will bring the dream to its ultimate realization.

The unfolding of this emphasis upon conservative and fundamental theological training must be followed in the history of Asbury College, for it is in the midst of this history that Asbury Theological Seminary ultimately came into being. As Abel observes in his *Historical Study*, page 78,

> There is little or no evidence of reaction against religious liberalism in the founding of the school, but as the rise of 'Modernism' from the turn of the century began to effect the colleges and seminaries of this country, Asbury College assumed the new obligation of defending the conservative, orthodox position in general without lessening its stress upon experiential holiness.

Undoubtedly, the increasing concern about the rise of modern heresy and infidelity among many colleges and universities became an important factor in the preparation of theological educational opportunities under conservative and orthodox leadership. As it will be seen presently, this leadership found one of its chief rallying points in Asbury College.

The coming of Henry Clay Morrison to the presidency of Asbury College in 1910 did not alter the character or purpose of the institution from that which it had been from the time of its founding by John Wesley Hughes. The number of its pre-theological students had increased across the years, and thus by some came to be looked upon as primarily an institution for the training of ministers. Morrison sought to clarify this at the beginning of his administration by affirming that Asbury was essentially a liberal arts college, though in the course of the years it had served the church well in preparing many young people to serve as pastors, missionaries, teachers, and evangelists. By 1913 the College had established two formal courses of theological training: one of lesser academic requirement granting a certificate, and the second of higher academic requirement granting a theological diploma in connection with the bachelor of arts degree. Early in 1915 it was announced that the College would offer a complete theological seminary course, but this did not actually materialize until eight years later when the organization of Asbury Theological Seminary was ultimately achieved.

Continued progress was made toward this official founding in 1923. In 1920 President Morrison publicized his expectation that out of the theological department of the College there would soon be realized a graduate seminary. He also affirmed his desire for higher academic standards in asserting that the several theological courses, which were worthy of being credited toward a post-graduate degree, were not to be used for credit toward the bachelor of arts degree. This aspiration of Dr. Morrison was shared by many who were closely associated with him in the work of the church and in the leadership of Asbury College. Early in 1923 an article appeared in *The Pentecostal Herald* (April 23, 1923) entitled "The Theological Seminary." In this Morrison described his purpose more fully and wrote, "We are working hard and faithfully for the new and advanced step in Asbury College in the form of a full-fledged theological seminary."

The days of the birth of Asbury Theological Seminary were times of theological confusion, struggle and controversy especially within Methodism. The liberal (unorthodox) theologians were denying certain basic foundations of Christian faith; and were beginning to preach and publicize such heretical ideas abroad especially within the church. On the other hand the conservative (orthodox) theologians were determined to preserve the foundational truths of the Christian faith, and sought to establish themselves for the defense of "the faith once delivered to the saints."

The trial of Professor H. G. Mitchell, of the Department of Old Testament in Boston University School of Theology, for heretical influences in his teaching, marks the beginning of a long and bitterly fought contest among theologians and churchmen in general. This began as early as a few years before the turn of the century, but soon after the close of the First World War the struggle was much intensified and widespread. By 1925 conservative organizations began to appear. Under the leadership of Dr. Harold Paul Sloan, one of the great scholars and theologians of his generation, the Methodist League for Faith and Life was organized. Its purpose was to reaffirm the vital and eternal truths of the Christian religion, such as the inspiration of the Scriptures, the deity of Jesus, His virgin birth, etc.

Since this conflict was primarily theological, it was greatly concerned with the substance of theological instruction. It involved the curriculum of the theological seminaries and also the conference course of study, which many young preachers who did not have opportunity of attending seminary were, required to pursue. The center of debate, therefore, was usually at the point of theological training, believing that as the people were taught and led by the ministry, so they would be established during succeeding generations.

As a part of this conservative movement the Evangelical Methodist League was formed under the leadership of Henry Clay Morrison in 1923. While this league was organized as a very practical and popular movement, it was also quite theological in nature. At least a part of its purpose was to conserve the orthodox teachings of the church. It sought to accomplish this by safeguarding the theological instruction of the ministry. The League also had another worthy promoter of the cause in the person of the Reverend Dr. George W. Ridout, one of the best-read religious leaders of his generation. Dr. Ridout came in 1922 to teach in the Theological Department of Asbury College. Morrison and Ridout at this time-shared very closely in the conviction that the church was in considerable danger, not only because of liberal and unscriptural teachings within many theological seminaries, but also because of the evidences of declining zeal within the church in general.

It was, therefore, at this time when Asbury Theological Seminary was about to be born, as it had been about thirty-three years earlier at the birth of Asbury College, that one sees the expressed concern for a positive constructive affirmation of the Christian faith as it had been lived and preached in apostolic Christianity. In neither case was it a negative reaction against the religious *status quo*, but rather a genuine reform movement, which is seeking to purify the Christian community and to make the church in its generation the most vital and redemptive force in all the world.

The purpose of such an institution, which the founding fathers of the Seminary had in mind, is no doubt best expressed in the fourth article of incorporation, section D., which reads as follows:

> The business, nature, and purpose of the corporation among other things shall be, to maintain the corporation of a Theological Seminary for the promotion of Theological Education. It will be the object of this Seminary to prepare and send forth a well-trained, sanctified, Spirit-filled, evangelistic ministry. This Seminary will emphasize in its teaching the divine inspiration and infallibility of the Holy Scripture, the Virgin Birth, Godhead, Vicarious Sufferings, and bodily resurrection of our Lord Jesus Christ. The instruction of this Seminary will fully recognize the fallen estate of mankind, the necessity of individual regeneration, the witness of the Spirit, the remains of the carnal nature, and entire sanctification as a definite second work of grace subsequent to regeneration. The instruction in this Seminary will conform fully to the Wesleyan interpretation of the Scripture. The instructors in this institution will guard with jealous care against any sort of teaching in sympathy with modern liberalism.

We see pretty clearly, then, that Asbury Theological Seminary was the result of an evolutionary process which had been increasing in force during most of the lifetime of Asbury

College since its founding in 1890. The need for a graduate school of theological education within the Wesleyan Arminian school of thought had become increasingly apparent through all these years from 1890 to 1923. The need for a theological school, which could maintain the faith against the inroads of modern liberalism, was certainly an important consideration in the founding of the Seminary. It was the conviction of some of the leaders that because many of the graduates of Asbury College had no choice but to attend a seminary where the faith of the fathers was neither honored or preserved, the establishing of a conservative and orthodox seminary had become a crying need.

Thus it was early in 1923 that President Morrison called a group of representative faculty, including Dr. Fred Halsey Larabee, Dean of the College, Professors Ridout, Harrison, Maxie, Hawkins, and Reynolds, to consider the plan for such a seminary. After considerable discussion, and the sure recognition of divine guidance, which had been sought through earnest prayer, there seemed to be a unity of assurance, and President Morrison speaking for the group declared that there would be a seminary and it would open its doors in September of that year (1923). This official beginning of Asbury Theological Seminary may appear to be like the decision of one man, but it must be remembered that Morrison is here giving expression to the desire of the group. He is the one who is called by them to give leadership to this movement. Several of these men had strongly urged him toward the realization of this end, so that he was acting in their behalf and with their full consent. The administration of the Seminary was for the most part under the personal supervision of Morrison during several of the early years. While it has certainly been wise that such autocratic administration should not be continued indefinitely, undoubtedly for a time it was a part of the good providence of God. There is perhaps a significant parallel between the relation of Wesley to the Methodist movement of the eighteenth century and that of Morrison to the establishment of Asbury Theological Seminary. In both cases the relation between the man and the movement is temporary, and in both cases there are strong evidences of a good providence of God.

At the beginning of the first academic year Dr. Fred Halsey Larabee who was then Dean of the College was appointed also Dean of the Seminary. Through a sudden and peculiar series of events, the Reverend Frank Paul Morris who had been a pastor in Indiana Methodism for a good number of years was called by Morrison to teach theology. Before this first year had ended Dr. Morris had been asked to assume the responsibilities of the Dean in order to allow Dean Larabee to give more attention to the College. Morris recognized this office as only an acting deanship for one year, and in 1924, at his own recommendation and by the appointment of the President, the office of Dean was filled by Dr. Larabee. The coming of these two outstandingly good and scholarly men was another evidence of the remarkable providence of God in the earliest days of the Seminary. Dr. Larabee's work as teacher in the field of New Testament Language and Literature, and his wise and efficient leadership as Dean have made his a name written in large letters upon the minds and hearts of many students who have gone into all the world to preach the glorious Gospel of the Son of God.

The timely appearance of Dr. Morris to become the example as well as the teacher of the revelation of God to men marked a very significant day in the life of this young institution. His department of Practical Theology and Homiletics became a mighty influence in shaping the lives of scores of theological students according to the divine pattern. It has been most fitting that the second building to be owned by the Seminary, and in which for a time the entire business of the institution was carried on, should bear the honored name of Larabee-Morris Hall.

Chapter 3
Growing Up

History reveals that very frequently the progress of a great movement or the establishment of a mighty institution is little else than the lengthening of the shadow of a great man. The Christian missionary enterprise of the first century in a very important sense is the prolongation of the shadow of the apostle Paul. The reawakening of the apostolic faith in Western Europe in the early sixteenth century, and the subsequent revivals, which have followed around the world for more than four centuries, are in a very real sense the lengthening shadow of Martin Luther.

To be sure, the history of Asbury Theological Seminary expresses this in a much lesser degree than the above illustrations, but the same principle is manifest in the relationship between the early and continuing life of Asbury Theological Seminary and its founder and first president, the Rev. Dr. Henry Clay Morrison. Certainly this theological and evangelical institution, both from the earliest times and through all the years even to the present, has born much of the image and likeness of this commanding leader. Morrison's great love for God and compassion for man has dominated the life of Asbury Seminary through these several generations. These spiritual qualities of a man so clearly called by God compelled him to take to the road in many states and around the world much as his spiritual ancestor, Francis Asbury, had done a century before. Yes, the spirit, thought, and purpose of Morrison have been so kept alive in this institution with a world vision and a great compassion for the lost, that the same prophetic word, which he preached, is being proclaimed by Asburians to the ends of the earth.

As has been observed in an earlier chapter the administration of President Morrison was often carried on, of necessity, with lack of concern about representation. Official acts were sometimes the decision of one man. It is good to know that these independent decisions were for the most part owned and blessed by God. The difficulties encountered by the founder were severe and numerous. Even after two years the Seminary found itself without any building specifically for its own use. At this time Morrison affirmed his intention to achieve certain objectives. These were all of a material nature, but were very essential for the proper expression of the spiritual life of the new institution. These included provision for faculty housing, a more adequate endowment fund, a loan fund for all ministerial students, and more adequate student housing.

The growth of student enrollment during the early years was rapid, reaching an annual average of nearly two hundred. However, the accommodated academic standard maintained by the Seminary at this time had much to do with this large enrollment. From 1923 to 1938 college juniors and seniors were allowed to choose among their elective courses enough theological subjects to satisfy, the requirements of the Seminary for the first year of theological studies. Asbury was not alone in this practice since it had been quite a general procedure among seminaries of the South. It was shortly to be discontinued however, and as the academic standards were raised, and after several urgent recommendations of Dean Larabee that the Seminary seek constantly for the highest and best in scholarship and efficiency, the trustees authorized the granting of a B. D. degree only upon the completion of three full years of graduate theological study after one had been awarded the A. B. degree or its equivalent.

The basic course offerings of the Seminary as presented in its original catalogue (1922-23) included most of the theological disciplines, which have remained as a part of the curriculum. These were:

1) Old Testament Language and Literature
2) New Testament Language and Literature
3) Biblical Theology
4) Systematic Theology
5) Historical Theology
6) Apologetics and Christian Ethics
7) Practical Theology
8) Missions
9) Church Music and Hymnology
10) Expression

A lasting emphasis has been placed upon the Biblical studies which has sought to encourage a careful and scholarly as well as a devotional pursuit of the Holy Scriptures. In the Bulletin of the Seminary for 1923-24 it is affirmed that

> The Bible as the Word of God is the fundamental text-book in Asbury Theological Seminary. Our aim is to give students a comprehensive acquaintance with its contents, and from the spiritual standpoint, so to interpret the Word of God that our graduates shall be thoroughly grounded as believers and preachers of the Bible... We hold, no matter how well trained a student may be in literary

matters, in theology, in apologetics, and no matter how zealous he may be in Christian work or what qualifications he may have, if he is not grounded in the Word of God, his personal safety as a Christian and his value as a religious leader is imperiled. The Bible must be our great textbook and the Holy Spirit our teacher.

The process of maturing and of achievement of some measure of independence from the College were in evidence as early as 1926. This year at the May meeting of the Board of Trustees the following was adopted:

Resolved, by the Board of Trustees of this corporation… that it would be to the great interest and advantage of this corporation to establish, maintain, and equip, as a separate and distinct department of its business, a "Theological Seminary" for the purpose hereinafter stated; and further that there be and is hereby established, as a separate and distinct department of business of this Corporation a "Theological Seminary" to be known as "Asbury Theological Seminary," to be maintained, supported, and equipped by this Corporation, and to have a Theological faculty for the purpose of giving theological instruction, training, and education to those of the students of this Corporation and College, desiring to equip themselves to enter the ministry; but that such department and faculty is to be under the control and direction of the Board of Trustees of this Corporation; and for the foregoing purposes, that this Corporation shall exercise the power granted and conferred upon it by its articles and amended articles of incorporation, of conferring proper degrees in Theology under the rules and regulations and upon such conditions as may be prescribed by this Board, or its executive Committee, with the approval and consent of this Board, on graduates of said "Seminary," as well as the power of conferring honorary degrees in Theology, upon clergymen or ministers.

This action of the Trustees gave to Asbury Theological Seminary a measure of independence and the right of a separate legal status. It was no longer simply a department of the College, but rather a distinct theological school. Its board of control was still one with that of the College and yet it had an official independent existence, and the responsibility to carry forward its theological program as an independent corporation.

Further evidence of significant advance may be noted toward the end of the third decade of this century. A greater confidence seemed to possess the minds of both faculty and administration. Likewise, there was an increased attraction toward this institution, which is reflected, in a substantial rise in student enrollment. The registrar's record shows that the total number of new students enrolling in the five-year period from 1926-30 was one hundred and ninety-one. But these days of advance and success were not allowed to go unchallenged. Late in 1929 Dr. Morrison was brought nigh unto death by an over-worked and weakened body. Though the Seminary was now in some respects well organized, in that some of the responsibilities were being assumed by co-laborers, yet its life was so much dependent upon that peculiar and vigorous leadership which the founder was able to give. And as it has so often happened for the people of God, in the good providence of God a clear miracle of healing was performed by the Great

Physician. The founder was restored to a new life, and he bore a deep conviction that God had restored him for the specific task of seeing the Seminary through another crisis and of giving further direction to its life in the years ahead.

Morrison immediately upon his restoration of physical health was keenly aware of the call of God to a specific mission, namely that of giving his major attention to the progress of the Asbury Seminary. An important instrument in this campaign was *The Pentecostal Herald* of which he was the editor. Through this medium and also as a result of his numerous and extensive journeys in his campaigns of evangelism and missions, the president of the Seminary had become the most representative and influential leader of the Holiness Movement in America. Likewise, his place in this movement as a unifying force was undoubtedly greater than any other one man. This relationship was of very great importance to the Seminary, especially at this critical time in its history. Through the pages of *The Herald* the appeal was presented to many thousands of its readers who had complete confidence in the editor and in the relevance of the mission, which he was seeking to accomplish. Small amounts of support came from many consecrated people of limited material resources. They came not only from many sections of America but also from other parts of the world wherever the knowledge of the work of Henry Clay Morrison had been made known. His philosophy indicated a deep spiritual wisdom, for he believed that a dollar each from a thousand people, who were giving sacrificially and meaningfully, was better than a thousand dollars from one person. The editor also believed that a plan, which would enlist the attention and prayer and service of a very large constituency, would build a far more lasting foundation for the new Seminary. This has continued to be the policy of the administration across the years. The keen sense of its utter dependence upon God by means of the prayers, love, gifts and service of a great host of His people has been preserved until the present. While the need for the building of a permanent endowment has been recognized, and through the years has been increasingly accomplished, the conviction that Asbury Theological Seminary has properly belonged to the people of God has been freely recognized by its leaders. Again, it is not a matter of either-or, but one of both-and, a large constituency of humble, praying, consecrated, giving people and a substantial endowment, both entirely under the control of, and all for the glory of God.

The financial support of the Seminary became involved with the academic maturing and also with the relationship between the College and Seminary. A committee was therefore chosen to prepare Articles of Incorporation for Asbury Theological Seminary. These were approved June 4, 1931. They indicate the great care and concern which the Administration, Trustees, and Faculty demonstrated in order to safeguard the original purpose for which the Seminary was established. (See Supplement A, page 95). It was believed that because of the increasing number of theological students; there would be those within the supporting constituency who would desire to contribute specifically to the task of preparing young men for the ministry. Thus it seemed wise to take further steps in separating the two institutions. It was affirmed that the independence of the Seminary should in no wise decrease the conviction that both institutions were continuing to serve a common cause, and that the sense of togetherness must be preserved.

The advance of the Seminary was seriously delayed again in 1933, first, because of the general financial depression of the late twenties and early thirties, and second, through the failure of the health of the Rev. Louis R. Akers, which caused him to resign as President of Asbury College. This brought about the issuing of a call to Morrison to return to the College as acting President in addition to his duties as President of the Seminary. With a great confidence in the healing and sustaining power of God, and in spite of being well into his seventies (he was then seventy-six) and already carrying far more than the load of a normal young man, he accepted this call from the College and proceeded with great enthusiasm and vigor to go forward with God in this task. The indebtedness of the College had reached nearly a half million, and this in a time of great economic depression and of financial uncertainty. It was at this time that Morrison conceived the idea of the Victory League, a plan that was given by God during a period of earnest prayer and of definite leadership of the Holy Spirit. The League was almost immediately a success; and again through the instrumentality of *The Pentecostal Herald*, large numbers of people from many parts of the world responded to the appeal to save the College from bankruptcy and make possible the continuation of the Seminary.

The election of the Rev. Dr. Zachary Taylor Johnson as the Executive Vice President of Asbury College was done at the suggestion of President Morrison. This relieved the latter of many administrative responsibilities and enabled him to spend most of his time in the field in behalf of both institutions. He also continued to speak to thousands of friends through *The Herald*. During the first year of this arrangement (1934-35) about fifty-three thousand dollars were raised. Likewise, in the fall of 1935 the revival of emphasis upon the general Thanksgiving Offering brought as much as forty-four thousand dollars. The debt of $456,000.00, which threatened the life of both institutions in 1934, had been completely liquidated within less than five years. These were indeed critical days in which both Asbury institutions were struggling for their lives. But now that a great victory had been obtained, a new day of challenge and opportunity presented itself. One of the demands of this new day was the quest for accreditation. Before the end of the first decade in the life of the Seminary this question of adequate preparation for academic recognition became a primary concern. The story of this quest will be told in a later chapter.

Chapter 4
Maturing Youth

The quest for accreditation had been pursued by both of the Asbury institutions for several years, and the possibility of achieving this objective was involved in the relationship, which the two schools had to each other. In 1939 the College was informed that its membership in the Southern Association of Colleges, Universities, and Secondary Schools was dependent upon its meeting of two additional requirements. One of these had to do with endowment. The other made necessary a complete separation from the Seminary. The law of the Association required that any professional school operated by a college must have its accreditation independent of the parent institution. It was clear then that a complete separation of administration and control was necessary for the best interest of all concerned, and also for the future success and usefulness of both the College and Seminary.

The process of separation was slow and complicated. One of the first steps was the formation of an agreement, between the College and Seminary Trustees, providing for a new building in the process of construction to be leased by the College to the Seminary. This building was originally known as Talbott Hotel, it being established as a part of the James Neblett Talbott Endowment Fund. The purpose had been to provide a hotel adjoining the College campus for the purpose of entertaining visitors. To lease this building for Seminary operation seemed to be a happy solution for a part of the problem of accreditation. Thus at the suggestion of President Morrison, this building was rented to the Seminary for two years. This put Asbury Theological Seminary in the most completely independent situation that it had thus far known. It provided a separate campus as well as its own faculty, curriculum, and board of control.

To be sure this increased independence was a mark of progress, yet it entailed serious problems. It placed the young institution in a rented building and without sufficient funds to maintain its operation. It also left the Seminary with a drastic reduction in faculty, there being only four professors. This caused the curriculum to be seriously curtailed even though the few members of the faculty were willing to assume the responsibility of teaching many additional subjects. These conditions further delayed the hope of being accredited, and the administration upon the recommendation of Dean Larabee wisely refrained for a time from presenting its case to the accrediting agency.

On the other hand, it must be remembered that in spite of the fact that this bold step of separation was costly, there were compensations. These are certain signs of the steady and sure progress, which was being accomplished in the life of the Seminary. The Dean reported the year 1939-40 as one of the finest in all of Asbury's history. He noted a distinct improvement in student attitude and morale and an increased sense of academic dignity because of participating in a uniquely theological graduate course of study.

After the Seminary had rented the Talbott Hotel for two years, at the suggestion of Dr. Zachary Taylor Johnson, who had been elected President of Asbury College on May 27, 1940, a plan of property settlement was worked out between the two institutions. During the years of President Morrison's administration, in fact during the entire lifetime of the Seminary up to 1940, many of the funds, which had been raised, had been for both schools and had therefore been invested for the interest of both. Morrison Hall on the College campus had been designated as the "Seminary Building" and had been used in large measure for theological purposes. After considerable discussion between the two boards it was agreed that in exchange for all the material holdings to which it had right on the College campus the Seminary would be granted the Talbott Hotel. It was in this single building that Asbury Seminary was to continue for a few years its new life as an independent school of theological learning.

In the course of these days of widespread discussion about separation it is of interest to note that there was very serious thought entertained concerning the possibility of relocating the Seminary. There were those who believed that important advantages would accrue by locating near one of the larger cities. The suggested city, which was named in the plan, was Louisville, Kentucky.

There was a robust enthusiasm, which marked the life of this youthful institution. Clearly it was giving evidence of severe growing pains. The body was finding it very difficult to grow as rapidly as the spirit. Very soon the limited space of Talbott Hall (later known as Larabee-Morris Hall) was crowded far beyond its capacity for operation of all the Seminary functions.

The President of the Seminary at this time was being encouraged not only by the generous responses, which he had been receiving from his numerous appeals to *The Herald* family throughout many states and some other lands, but also by the solid and sacrificial support, which came from the Board of

Trustees. The minutes of this Board under date of May 31, 1941, indicated genuine optimism and loyalty. The minutes read:

> After some remarks concerning the growth and development of the Seminary and the importance of its place in the religious life of America, and the necessity of its perpetuation, Dr. J. C. McPheeters made a motion which was seconded by Dr. H. G. Ryan, that a movement to be known as the H. C. Morrison Living Endowment Fund for Asbury Theological Seminary be instituted... This movement met with great acclaim and it is believed that through this medium, quite a sum of money can be secured annually to assist in carrying on this great work.

In the spring of 1941 a public proposal was made to erect an apartment building for married students, many of whom were then attending the Seminary but had arranged for their own housing in the local community. The immediate plans for building were hindered by the war and the scarcity of materials. Morrison nevertheless kept publicizing and making repeated appeals through *The Herald* for the building of a great evangelical and evangelistic Seminary to meet the crying needs of that day. His building dream was enlarged to include, in addition to the proposed apartment, an administration building, which would become the center of activity. This was also to be the initial unit of the Morrison Memorial Quadrangle.

In *The Pentecostal Herald* for November 19, 1941, Morrison proclaimed the heart of his conviction that he should establish such a Seminary when he said:

I should not undertake the building up of this Seminary, but for the fact that I feel it is one of the greatest needs in the world; that we should have a theological Seminary in teaching and purpose, in perfect accord with the spirit and message of John Wesley and his co-workers, in the kindling of the greatest religious revival in the history of the Christian Church.

The conclusion of the first presidential administration for Asbury Theological Seminary came with the passing and triumph of the highly esteemed and well-beloved Henry Clay Morrison. He had commanded with the hand of a great master the affairs of this new Seminary through the first nineteen years of its life. These had been years of numerous and severe difficulties, but out of them all with a full recognition of divine guidance and supernatural assistance, the wisdom of Morrison had led.

As has been observed in an earlier chapter, the life and nature of this Seminary has been very closely identified with and under the control of its founder and first president. Because of this identity and consequent dependence of the institution upon the leadership of a single individual, there came in this period of transition a special opportunity for pessimists to conclude that the day of Asbury would now soon close. But such was not the case. Through a period of two decades the holy fire of Morrison's spirit had started flames in the lives of a goodly number, some of who were capable of forceful leadership, and others who were committed to a faithful support. In addition to this it was clear that God had His man to succeed in this line of noble men. Dr. Julian C. McPheeters, on April 3, 1942, was elected as the Acting President, and at the next regular meeting of the Trustees (May 30, 1942) he was elected the second President of Asbury

Theological Seminary. McPheeters was likewise chosen to succeed Morrison as editor of *The Pentecostal Herald,* which enabled him to maintain the fine unity between Asbury and *The Herald*, which had been so effectively held by his predecessor. It was President McPheeters himself who said that the passing of such a preacher-saint and dynamic personality as the beloved Morrison gave the impression that a great star had fallen from its place in the sky. It caused one to tremble at the loss. But here, too, was one who stood ready to invest his all and his best in the mission to which God had called. The Seminary therefore under the leadership of the new President was to continue to advance, as it did often through stormy ways, but ever onward to ultimate victory.

Early in 1943 the plans for the Henry Clay Morrison Memorial Administration Building were given to the architect. These plans, though not the name, had been revealed from the dreams of Dr. Morrison. His widow, more familiarly known as Aunt Bettie who had co-operated so effectively with her husband in building the Seminary, had so shared in all these dreams that she was well able to describe them to the architect. They were suggested somewhat in detail, including a library, lobby, dean's office, chapel, and prayer room. The two upper floors were to serve as classrooms and additional dormitory space.

Even in the midst of preparation for new buildings the growth of the student body was such as to require even larger plans than had been anticipated. By the fall of 1944 President McPheeters, with the executive committee of the Board, had recommended in addition to the administration building, a chapel to accommodate five hundred people, and a library of 50,000 volumes. In addition to these plans the architect suggested the provision for a splendid dining room on the ground floor from the rear of the Administration Building.

The scaling of these plans was effected on October 23, 1945, in the groundbreaking ceremonies for the Morrison Memorial Quadrangle. This was a day of supreme joy for Mrs. Henry Clay Morrison who had invested so much of her life and talent in order to make real that which her sainted husband had dreamed. A second event of outstanding significance upon that October day was the decision of the Board to proceed with the building of a twenty-four unit family apartment in process with the Morrison Quadrangle. These were days of destiny both for God's work and for His servants. Only three days after her official act of inaugurating the construction of the Administration Building, Mrs. Morrison suffered a heart attack and entered the life triumphant early the next month (November 8, 1945). In high esteem of her faithful and courageous labors in behalf of the young men entering the Christian ministry, the Board of Trustees designated the new apartment building the Elizabeth Morrison Memorial Hall. To this day the building is known among the members of the Asbury family as "The Bettie Morrison Hall," a name that seems to keep forever alive the universal respect and genuine love, which Asburians hold for Aunt Bettie.

The Administration Building, which was the first and central structure of the Quadrangle, was opened for use in the fall of 1947, and the "Aunt Bettie" apartment house was ready for occupancy one year later.

In spite of these rather unusual material accomplishments, the physical advances of the Seminary seemed never to be able to keep abreast of the increase in personnel. The interest in and enthusiasm for this young theological graduate school was reflected in a large increase in student enrollment nearly every year. In 1946 temporary provision was made for additional housing by converting several old dwellings into apartments and by procuring several

Government surplus trailers. This made provision for the housing of about fifty more students, but even this was quite inadequate. And so the demand continued, and the Seminary continued to be embarrassed by its success. A summary of material achievement was reported by President McPheeters in the spring of 1950. This was seen in the investment of $800,000 represented by two major buildings with an adequate central heating plant, and nine small buildings. Issuing an appeal for the second phase in order to erect the chapel and the library another $600,000 was asked. This amount was to be realized in a relatively brief time through the sacrifice and loyalty of many friends of the institution. In addition to all this, early in 1951 the Seminary began the erection of brick duplex apartments for students with families. Two large sections of land toward the edge of Wilmore had been purchased for this purpose and about forty units have thus far been built.

It was believed that for several years in the late forties the Seminary lost as many as fifty to a hundred students because of the lack of housing facilities. The fact remains, however, that during the forties there was a steady growth in enrollment and up to the middle of the century it had reached nearly four hundred. This flood time of interest and full enrollment was maintained until the years of the early fifties and the "times of Israel's troubles" when the loss of academic accreditation was sustained because of internal theological disturbances. But this story will be more fully told in a subsequent chapter. It may be to the point of our present consideration, however, to observe that through all these handicaps in the loss of accreditation the Seminary never suffered any damaging loss in student enrollment; and also, that even though there was considerable divergence of theological opinion among the faculty, except for the resignation of one professor, the faculty has remained and has continued in its service more effective than ever.

Chapter 5
Out of Weakness—Strength

At the beginning of the second half of the twentieth century Asbury Theological Seminary was confronted with several serious difficulties. There continued a financial debt of about a quarter of a million dollars. The loss of accreditation had reduced the student enrollment so that It was estimated to be costing the Seminary at least thirty thousand dollars per year because of the decline in tuition income. The constant rise in the size of the average student's family required enlarged housing facilities. The constant rise in the cost of living required some increase in the remuneration for the faculty, staff, and general employees of the institution. One of the most insistent demands of the accrediting agency was that there be an immediate increase in faculty salaries. These at the time were among the very lowest of all the theological institutions in the nation.

With these numerous pressures increasing, the administration of the Seminary was also aware that in order to meet the general operating expenses of the institution each dollar that was paid for his education by the student, at least one additional dollar had to be sought from voluntary contributions. There was no endowment or denominational church board to underwrite these increasing costs.

Indeed there were seasons of very great darkness even as late as the early years of the fifties. President McPheeters tells of such a dark night when financial obligations were much beyond the institution's resources. It seemed to him for a while that there was no answer and no place to turn for help. But then God, as in a sudden moment of inspiration and guidance by the revealed presence of His Holy Spirit, indicated the place where the necessary money could be found. This was the much-needed light in the midst of temporary darkness. A sufficient loan was obtained from the one whom God had brought to the attention of President McPheeters and the emergency was met.

It is quite evident that during these days of pressure and unusual major difficulties many valuable lessons were being taught in the school of experience and by the instruction of God the Holy Spirit. It was during these years that the Asbury family was being united in the bond of love and a renewed unity of intercession. It was a time when the faculty, staff, and student body came to a fresh realization that the continued success of the Seminary depended more upon God than man. The truth declared by the prophet when he uttered the words, "not by might, nor by power, but by my Spirit, saith the Lord," were frequently expressed on campus, and more firmly believed and more generally applied.

The encouragement to a deeper and broader prayer life was recommended and led by the president and faculty. New emphasis was placed upon the revival of the general prayer life movement, which was meeting with considerable success not only in America but also in other parts of the world. One of the major thrusts of this movement was the work, which had lately been begun by the General Board of Evangelism of The Methodist Church. Dr. Harry Denman, the Executive Secretary of this Board, had expressed such great conviction for the need of such a revival of prayer life to undergird the work of evangelism and world missions that it was ultimately established within the General Board as a distinct department. One who shared much of the same conviction with Dr. Denman was the Rev. Thomas A. Carruth, pastor of the Broad Street Methodist Church at Hattiesburg, Mississippi. In 1953 Dr. Carruth came to the General Board of Evangelism to begin a work, which finally developed into The Prayer Life Movement.

Much of the spiritual life developed at Asbury at this time was closely identified with this general prayer life movement. Organizations were initiated through which the fruit of prayer could be more effectively provided to meet the needs of the world. Each academic year was opened with a prayer convocation. This consisted of two major parts. First, a faculty retreat was conducted in an off-campus, quiet, secluded environment for a period of two days. The purpose of this experience was to see and know God more intimately, to understand and love one another more devotedly, and to comprehend and accept the mission, which God had assigned. The second part of the convocation was another two-day period in which faculty, staff, and students participated together. A twenty-four hour chain of prayer was established in which several hundred participated and many significant spiritual victories were achieved. Specific objects of intercession were presented beginning with personal, institutional, and community needs near at hand. However, this list of needs was extended beyond the limitation of community, state, and nation until the ends of the world were touched by the spirit of deep concern and prevailing prayer. Such instructions in a school of prayer and participation in a life of prayer have led many theological students into a far more fruitful ministry.

Many other encouragements to the prayer life have been offered. The prayer vigils have been a continuing source of divine strength. This vigil is kept through an eighteen-hour period each day from six in the morning until twelve midnight. The center of this vigil is the Haskins-Luce Prayer Chapel. Here requests for prayer come daily from all over the nation and from many other nations throughout the world. Across the last decade a remarkable confidence in the effectiveness of the prayers of Asbury Theological Seminary has been increasingly expressed. This has helped to keep the need of the world before the eyes and the burden of the world upon the heart of the personnel of this Seminary.

Other encouragements to strengthen the life of prayer and increase its fruitfulness were the forming of prayer cells and prayer partners. These prayer-sharing experiences were multiplied by dozens, and many have witnessed to the spiritual significance that such a discipline has had upon their lives.

The mid-week general prayer hour is also an important contribution to the total life of the Seminary community. The strengthening of this fellowship in prayer is in large measure due to the leadership of President Stanger. The appeal of the President has been to increase the sense of community throughout the whole Asbury family. One of the principle means of accomplishing this has been a full participation of all members in the mid-week prayer hour.

Days of special intercession have frequently been called by the spiritual life committee. Such occasions are planned to reinforce the prayer power by a greater concentration of participants in each of the twenty-four hours through the day and night, and also by a concentration upon some special need or crisis in the life of the institution, the church or the world.

Chapter 6
Material Advance

The material manifestation of an institution is normally the measure of its real life. Though there may be exceptions to this general rule, it usually follows that the physical form of an institution is the measure by which its life is expressed to the world. In the case of Asbury Theological Seminary the decade of the fifties was one of remarkable growth and expansion in material assets. It was a period when the inner life and spirit of the Seminary were demanding more numerous and adequate approaches to the outside world. It was as a youth maturing into adulthood. The life of the spirit was seeking more effective channels of expressing itself to the outer world.

This ever-expanding life at Asbury has been a continuing process across nearly all the years from the time of its birth. To be sure there have been times when the process was retarded, and momentarily it may have seemed to be at a complete standstill, but the decades bear witness to a certain and permanent success. Paul Abel in his very carefully written history of Asbury Theological Seminary concludes in the final paragraphs of that work that in all probability "The Seminary will never know another single period of development to equal that of the past decade" (1910-50). But the achievements of the fifties far exceeded those of the forties, and it would seem that such phenomenal growth would be exceeded in the decades yet in the future. The total assets of the Seminary were nearly quadrupled during the decade following 1950. The following records from the report of the business manager will indicate the great growth: Total assets in 1943 were $218,933; in 1950 they were $798,281; and in 1961 they were $4,098,019.

The first major building in the decade of the fifties was the erection of the Estes Chapel. This was completed in 1953 completely free of debt at a cost of $340,000 without furnishings. The chapel itself, which was dedicated to the glory of God on January 27, 1954, stands as a perpetual tribute to the Christian faith and munificence of Mr. and Mrs. Floyd Estes of Lansing, Michigan. The Haskins-Luce Prayer Chapel was made possible by a substantial gift from the Rev. and Mrs. Clayton Luce of Fort Lauderdale, Florida. The chapel organ was a gift in memory of Mr. Earl W. Savage, dedicated to the glory of God and as an enduring tribute to the love and affection of his wife, Mrs. Earl W. Savage, and their children, Mr. William E. Savage and Mrs. Dow N. Kirkpatrick. The Kresge Foundation whose beneficence helped to make the chapel possible presented its gift in memory of Mr. R. E. Olds, Christian philanthropist, pioneer automobile manufacturer, and champion of the American free enterprise system (1861-1950). Many other gifts and memorials were presented by members of the faculty, staff, and friends in order to completely furnish the interior.

The completion of the chapel became a real boost to the morale of the Seminary. Heretofore it had been necessary to use the sanctuary of the Methodist Church, which was some distance removed from the campus. The chapel with its amazing beauty and striking simplicity became the real center of the life of the Seminary community.

Another very urgent need was a building suitable for the housing of women students. The Ely-McIntire Hall for women was completed in 1959. This beautiful hall was made possible through substantial gifts from Mrs. H. B. (Grace) Ely, Dr. and Mrs. Warren G. McIntire, and other contributions.

Eighteen duplex dwellings for married students were erected as a part of the building program during the late fifties. These were found to offer very fine accommodations for the students and their families. They are simple in structure and economical in operation, but quite adequate and comfortable. The erection of these numerous duplex buildings was made possible by the generous gifts of Mr. William Broadhurst.

The Seminary's Largest Gift

Mr. B. L. Fisher of Martinsville, Virginia, was a devout Christian layman who regarded all of his possessions as a sacred trust from God. He regarded himself as a co-laborer with God in all of his business transactions. God blessed him as the owner and manager of the Lee Telephone Company, which had a small beginning, with only 15 telephones on the switchboard. As the company grew and developed across the years, he pledged all of the assets for the advancement of the Kingdom of God. At the time of his decease in 1955, the company had over 16,000 telephones on the switchboard.

In keeping with his lifelong commitment to God, Mr. Fisher directed by will practically his entire estate for Christian purposes. For a number of years previous to his decease, Mr. Fisher had served as a member of the Board of Trustees of Asbury Theological Seminary. Fifty per cent of his estate was directed to Asbury Theological Seminary. The Seminary realized over three million dollars in the sale of her share of the estate. The B. L. Fisher gift strengthened the financial structure of the Seminary beyond any single gift ever received.

As has been observed in an earlier chapter, the Seminary was from the beginning so closely identified with the life and public ministry of its founder and first president, that in the minds of many the institution was synonymous with the name of Henry Clay Morrison. It was he who had dreamed dreams from which Asbury had taken shape. It was he who had spent himself without reserve in order to support its young life. It was he who had come to the rescue of the youthful institution upon several occasions when its life was in very real danger.

But the rapid growth of the Seminary soon gave Morrison to know that he must have leadership assistance in all the areas of responsibility, which were related to its expanding life. The plan of appointing assistants to the President in the field had its origin here. Friends and supporters needed to be kept informed and encouraged to continue their undergirding of the institution in prayer, in service, and in gifts. The extent of this field was far beyond the reach of one man. The earliest helpers in this area were the Rev. E. L. Eaton and Mr. C. A. Lovejoy. These gave much of their time during the summer immediately before the opening of the Seminary in 1923 to turn the attention and interest of the largest possible number toward Asbury Seminary. The large number of *Herald* subscribers became a very responsive field of operation for these associates to the editor. In 1930 Morrison found a man in whom he had great confidence and for whose ability he had a very high regard. At this time he placed the Rev. Mr. H. H. McAfee in the field as a full-time representative. In 1944 Mr. Carl Ashe was employed as an assistant to the President and in 1949 the Rev. Mr. Robert Fraley was added to the staff of field associates. Mr. Fraley has served not only as assistant to the President, but from 1954 to 1962 as Director of Public Relations, and from 1962 to 1963 as Director of Stewardship.

The number of field assistants has increased with the growing demands of the institution. Between 1957 and 1962 there have been three full-time men employed in this ministry, the Rev. Mr. Lucas Cook, the Rev. Mr. Myron Z. Hovda, and Mr. Harry Naylor. During the same period eight part-time persons were so engaged. They are the Rev. Mr. Granger E. Fisher, the Rev. Mr. Dr. William J. Briggs, the Rev. Mr. Grove L. Armstrong, the Rev. Mr. Morgan, the Rev. Mr. Vernon Horney the Rev. Mr. Harold Millard, Mr. Robert E. Bellman, and Mr. Glenn W. Smith.

The success of these consecrated assistants has demonstrated their real value to the Seminary. Their work continues to be a means of spiritual as well as material enrichment to the many people across the world who are the friends of Asbury, as well as to the personnel of the Seminary itself.

Chapter 7
The Student Scholarship
Program and Alumni

This scholarship program of the Seminary was established, by President Henry Clay Morrison and has so strengthened its position across the years that it has become one of the institution's major bulwarks.

An organized plan of student scholarship aid was in operation as early as 1933. During this year the minutes of the Trustees show that there was a total of seventy-seven students who received financial assistance from this plan; twenty-one received $150 each, fifteen received $95 each, and forty-one received $50 each. This made a total of $7,000 provided by the Seminary for this purpose in one year. The next year the regular scholarships were reduced from $95 to $85 for each student.

During the next five years the number of scholarships given ranged from forty to sixty, making an average of fifty each year. In 1939 the minutes of the Trustees records that "forty-five full-time scholarships have been administered this year to our students, which would seem to indicate that there is no lessening of the interest of the donors to this worthy cause."

The Henry Clay Morrison Living Endowment Fund and Scholarship Program was confirmed and made permanent by the action of the Board of Trustees in 1941. At the suggestion of Dr. J. C. McPheeters, the regularity of these annual contributions to the scholarship fund was of such a guaranteed nature that it could be properly considered as interest being received from a considerable capital fund. Thus the reliance upon a "living endowment" consisted of the good will and deep concern of a very large and dependable constituency throughout the whole United States. This constituency had been established through the untiring work and leadership of *The Pentecostal Herald*, with Dr. Morrison as its founder and editor for nearly half a century.

Much of the responsibility for leadership in this scholarship fund was assumed by the wife of President Morrison, affectionately known among the members and friends of the Asbury family as "Aunt Bettie." In 1941 Mrs. Morrison obtained at least sixty scholarships, which provided enough for most of the students enrolled that year to participate in its benefits. This effective leadership was continued by Mrs. Morrison until the time of her death in 1945.

After the passing of Mrs. Morrison the work of directing the scholarship program was assigned to Dr. Julian C. McPheeters. During this decade of the forties the support of this fund increased in about the same proportion as the increase of the student enrollment. The amount contributed to this cause in 1950 exceeded $41,000. The provision for foreign student scholarships became an important development in terms of much greater responsibility and a greatly increased opportunity for service in theological education. First, the amount required for a scholarship to a student from another land was more than three times the amount required for a student residing in the United States. However, the enlarged opportunity of reaching many students from many nations has given great impetus to the scholarship program. According to a statement by President McPheeters the number of scholarships given to students from other lands during the forties and fifties ranged from twenty-five to thirty-five, and $50,000 to $65,000 per year has been raised through the scholarship program.

In his report to the Trustees, January 1963, President Stanger affirms:

> "Our Scholarship Program, which provides three hundred dollars in tuition scholarships for American students and nine hundred and sixty dollars for foreign students, continues to be one of the financial lifelines of the operational budget of the Seminary. During the past twelve months, more than fifty thousand dollars was received for the Scholarship Program."

This program has grown rapidly, not only in interest and numbers, but also in permanence. In 1963 there were twenty-one permanent scholarship endowments. Among these is the John Wesley Beeson Memorial Scholarship Fund, established by the family and friends of Dr. Beeson, himself a famous educator of the South. This fund has reached an amount in excess of one hundred thousand dollars and provides perpetually for four foreign student scholarships at the Seminary.

Permanent Scholarship Endowments:

The John Wesley Beeson Memorial Scholarship. Established by the family and friends of Dr. Beeson, famous educator of the South.

The Dora E. Baughman Memorial Scholarship Fund.

The Jefferson and Elizabeth Bentley Memorial Scholarship. Established by their daughter, Mrs. George Freitas.

The E. R. Boyd and Ella V. Boyd Memorial Scholarship. Established by Mr. and Mrs. E. R. Boyd.

The Letha U. Davis Memorial Scholarship.

The Richard Gordon Eddy Memorial Scholarship. Established by parents and friends.

The H. B. and Grace Ely Scholarship. Established by Mrs. Grace Ely.

The H. F. Ferguson Memorial Scholarship. Established by Mrs. H. F. Ferguson.

The Sila D. Foster Scholarship. Established by Mrs. Foster for the educating of young men for the Christian ministry.

The Richard Lawrence and Robert David McWhite Memorial Scholarship. Established by their parents, Mr. and Mrs. R. L. McWhite.

The Sadie Maude Jones Scholarship.

The Ulta Belle McDaniel Scholarship. Established by Miss Ulta Belle McDaniel.

The Ethel McPheeters Memorial Scholarship. Established by the family and friends of the Seminary on the occasion of her triumphal home going on January 28, 1956.

The Reverend and Mrs. W. T. Miller Scholarship.

Elizabeth W. Morgan Memorial Scholarship Fund. Established from the estate of Elizabeth W. Morgan.

The Reverend Earl Wesley Munson Foreign Student Scholarship Fund. Established by Martin S. Munson.

The Mrs. Margaret Peoples Memorial Scholarship. Established by her brother, Rev. A. D. Pilow.

The Hayden Pritchard Memorial Scholarship Fund.

The Gertrude and Somerville Memorial Scholarship. Established by the Reverend Norman Reginald Somerville.

The John R. Taylor Memorial Scholarship Fund. Established by Mrs. John R. Taylor.

The John Wilson Thome Scholarship. Established by his parents, Dr. and Mrs. M. T. Thome.

The Student Scholarship Program has demonstrated several areas of significant achievement. Basically, the financial undergirding, which it provides, makes it possible for many worthy students to pursue a theological education. Without such provision these students would be handicapped throughout their career. In addition to this achievement, however, there is one of greater spiritual significance. Each student who receives a scholarship is brought into a fellowship of prayer with the donor. This relationship is brought about by exchange of letters, and where it is possible by visitation, either on the campus or in the home of the donor. These prayer-fellowships between students and donors have produced many beautifully enriching and lasting results in the lives of all concerned in this scholarship program.

Alumni

There is no more accurate representation of the character of an educational institution than its alumni. This is the fruit it bears. This is that for which it has been created in order that it may produce. An institution is usually judged by the quality of its alumni. Just as a home is judged by the kind of children it sends into the nation, an institution helps to determine the kind of nation and world that is soon to be by the quality of its alumni.

The Seminary alumni were not organized as such during the first eighteen years of the school's history. This was due to the fact that the alumni of the College and of the Seminary both belonged to and participated in the College Alumni organization. It was Dean Larabee who suggested to the Seminary Trustees in 1941 that provision should be made for the organization of the alumni in order that there might be a more constructive and creative program in behalf of the Seminary in the outside world. The Dean's suggestions were not carried through until four years later. It was in the spring of 1945 that Mrs. Morrison appealed to the Rev. Mr. Don A. Morris of Michigan requesting that he take the initiative in bringing together the rapidly growing body of alumni for the purpose of performing a more effective service for their *alma mater*. This was done, and the preparatory committees worked throughout the year with such efficiency that the Seminary Alumni Association was formally organized during the Commencement of 1946. This Association has co-operated well with the Trustees, and they in turn have recognized the value of the alumni by choosing about one-third of their number from the Alumni Association.

Asbury Theological Seminary has taken justifiable pride in the number and character of her alumni. During the forty years of her life she has sent forth a company of 1,561 men and women trained for Christian work. These have gone forth into all the world to achieve great things for God and His Kingdom. More than two-thirds of this company has given themselves to full-time Christian service, 942 as ministers of the Gospel and 159 as missionaries. Members of Asbury's Alumni are providing spiritual leadership among forty-one denominations. The first twelve of these denominations in position of the highest numbers represented are as follows: Methodists 829, Free Methodist 232, Wesleyan Methodist 60, Evangelical United Brethren 48, Friends 33, Holiness (groups) 32, Nazarene 31, Evangelical Methodist 25, Christian and Missionary Alliance 19, Presbyterian 18, Pilgrim Holiness 15, Baptist 9.

Likewise, the geographical areas of service into which the graduates of the Seminary have gone is a study of considerable interest and significance. This company of loyal sons and daughters is now serving in forty-nine states, the District of Columbia, and in forty-two countries outside the United States of America.

The Alumni Association since the time of its organization has become increasingly a vital force in the support of the Seminary as well as a telling witness throughout much of the world.   One of its most significant material achievements was the raising of the funds for the establishing of the Frank Paul Morris, Chair of Christian Doctrine. This climaxed an all-out effort during a period of seven years; and it was an occasion of great joy and satisfaction to the whole Asbury family when at Commencement, May 28, 1963, the President of the Alumni, the Rev. Mr. Maurice W. Stevens, presented a check in the amount of two hundred thousand dollars to President Frank Bateman Stanger.

Chapter 8
Academic Progress

The years of the fifties for Asbury Theological Seminary were characterized by outstanding academic success. There may have been a certain measure of urgency in this direction because this was the period of long-continued struggle for reaccreditation, so that the academic advance may have been a kind of by-product. On the other hand, this progress in academic maturing during the fifties is simply one stage of long-time, general, determined effort on the part of this institution to achieve the very best in the finest expression of Christian scholarship.

President McPheeters was frequently heard to express great delight and satisfaction because of the wonderful providence, which had enabled him to assemble such a group of committed and academically prepared persons to the faculty. In 1949 the status of the faculty personnel showed a marked advance over the previous years. At this time there were sixteen with faculty status, ten of whom were full professors, of whom nine held earned doctor's degrees. By 1963 this same faculty had increased to twenty-five with full status, fifteen of whom were full professors, of whom fourteen held earned doctor's degrees. These fourteen hold degrees from nine institutions of higher learning including Harvard University, Drew University, State University of Iowa, Temple University,

Northern Baptist, Oregon State University, University of Cincinnati, University of Michigan, and University of Southern California. Denominationally there were nine families represented. These included Christian and Missionary Alliance, Evangelical United Brethren, Free Methodist, Friends, Methodist, Nazarene, United Missionary, United Presbyterian in U. S. A., and Wesleyan Methodist.

The student-faculty ratio from 1949 to 1963 likewise indicates a distinct improvement, advancing from 21.8 to 1 in the former year up to 13.4 to 1 in the latter year. Another phase of the academic achievement in evidence during the fifties was the building of endowments for the establishing of chairs in several departments. The Chair of Evangelism was established in 1955 by an annual gift of $7,500 by Mr. and Mrs. Sollie McCreless of San Antonio, Texas. This endowment has provided across the years for a full professor of evangelism, and for the general strengthening of the Seminary's position in this area of instruction through conferences, lectureships, and additional library facilities.

The campaign for launching the Frank Paul Morris Chair of Christian Doctrine was begun in 1956. The alumni of the Seminary sponsored this as a special project and in seven years had raised the complete amount, which was required, two hundred thousand dollars.

In 1959 the campaign for the Butler-Valade Chair of Biblical Theology was launched and more than $36,000 of this amount had been secured in 1962.

In keeping with the increased emphasis upon world missions especially during the years of the fifties, the Seminary early in 1963 had established a foundation by which a chair of missions was to be maintained. This was to be known as the

John Wesley Beeson Chair of Missions, and it was to be supported by an endowment of $200,000.

Library

The story of the library is also one of very great achievement and growth. Although as late as 1963 the librarian, Miss Susan Schultz, reported that the library was still in its infancy, the total number of volumes had grown from six hundred and fifty in 1940 to more than forty-four thousand in 1962. From the time when the Seminary was separated from Asbury College in 1939, the origin, development, organization, and housing of an adequate theological library seems to have been a matter of continuous concern. Upon the separation of the two schools the Seminary was practically without a library except for several hundred volumes, which were donated by the College. In order to meet this emergency an appeal was made by Dean Fred H. Larabee through *The Pentecostal Herald* for the contributions of certain theological volumes. The response to this appeal seems to have been gratifying, for within a year's time from the books thus obtained there were about three thousand highly desirable volumes, and these were organized and catalogued in such a way as to make them most useful to the students. A steady growth in the library facilities and in the number of volumes catalogued may be indicated by the following table:

1940	650 volumes
1950	28,000 volumes
1960	39,880 volumes
1963	44,022 volumes

By 1941 the library had increased three-fold and was subscribing to more than sixty periodicals. This collection, in charge of a student, was housed in a small basement room of the only Seminary building at that time. An important forward step at this time was a real attempt to adequately catalogue all the volumes.

At this time the Seminary was again urged to expand its library facilities by the American Association of Theological Schools. In order to comply in its quest for accreditation the Board of Trustees through its Executive Committee designated a minimum of five hundred dollars per year for new books. This annual influx of a thousand volumes soon over-taxed the housing space, and early in 1944 the library was moved to the alumni hall, an old store building rented from Asbury College at the comer of Lexington Avenue and College Street, just North of the Seminary building.

Further need for the expansion of library facilities was expressed by the accrediting association, and the Seminary designated ten thousand dollars for this purpose early in 1945. Soon thereafter an academically trained librarian was added to the faculty and within the year the volumes numbered ten thousand. The administration felt that this needed to be increased to fifteen thousand, but knew also that though the books were available the money to purchase them was not. An appeal was made to the alumni for a gift of forty dollars each. A good return from this was 'realized, as each member of the Senior Class of 1946 assumed a like amount. The success of this movement to establish an adequate theological library may be seen as an important turning point in the general academic success of the Seminary.

The reclassification of the library's holdings was accomplished in 1946. This followed the plan of the Union Theological Seminary. The embarrassment of further crowded housing in the alumni hall was relieved by the completion of the Henry Clay Morrison Administration Building. Into the lower ground floor level of this building the ever-growing library was moved in 1947, and this location furnished its most adequate provision for housing. Here at mid-century the Seminary made available to its rapidly growing student body more than twenty-eight thousand volumes, two thousand pamphlets, and two hundred and twenty-six periodicals.

Again in 1954 this enlarging library was requiring more space in order to function normally. The new home was found on the ground floor of Estes Chapel. Already in the minds of the administration, the faculty, and especially the librarian, the dream of a new and completely separate library building was becoming more and more vivid. The extreme urgency for the realization of this dream was expressed by the librarian, Miss Susan Schultz. In her report to the Board of Trustees, January 23, 1962, Miss Shultz asserted:

> Lack of adequate reader-space is only one cause for serious concern. Space in the workroom is now so limited that constant shifting is necessary and this eventually affects staff morale. From now on the administration of the library will become an increasingly expensive operation since constant shifting of materials will be necessary to make room for new acquisitions. It is quite obvious that some steps must soon be taken to remedy this situation.

While dreams were maturing into plans for the new library building the problem of insufficient space was intensified by a greater opportunity for the acquisition of many new volumes. In June of 1961 the Sealantic Fund made a grant of $875,000.00 for distribution among libraries of accredited seminaries during the next five years in amounts ranging from $500 to $3,000 on a matching basis for the purchase of books above the normal book budget. The officers of administration at Asbury voted full participation in the American Theological Library Association Library Development Program. This meant the purchase of six thousand dollars worth of books annually for three years, and this in addition to the regular annual book budget. This investment was required to be made in the procuring of standard works, and thus the position of the library was vastly strengthened. However, the acquisition of so many additional volumes naturally added to the seriousness of an already badly overcrowded space for proper library operations. The extremely urgent need for a new library called for action with the greatest possible haste.

On commencement day in May 1962, announcement was made that a large part of the funds for the new library building had been pledged. This was a contribution of $400,000.00 in connection with the sale of stock from the Fisher estate. It was designated that this gift was to go toward the construction of the B. L. Fisher Library Building. In November 1962, a carefully prepared plan for the new library building, representing the thought and work of Miss Susan Schultz and her assistants for several years, was presented to the architects. At the time of this writing it is anticipated that work will be begun late in 1963 and that the building will be ready for occupancy before the end of 1964.

Sabbatical Leaves for the Faculty

In 1955 the Seminary instituted a program of sabbatical leave for its faculty. The purpose of this provision was to encourage all faculty members to use this opportunity for intensive academic research. The use of such opportunity has been employed by most members of the faculty during the past eight years. Its enrichment in teaching ability and experience has been clearly in evidence, and this program has proved to be an ever increasing asset to the academic life of the entire Seminary.

The purpose of the institution in this area of scholarly competence was expressed by President Stanger in his report to the trustees in January of 1960: "Asbury Theological Seminary must be pertinent in its academic relationships. The members of our thoroughly-trained and highly-competent faculty must be encouraged, given opportunity, and aided in the regular production of works of scholarly research."

Foundations and Lectureships

In 1942, through the administration of Dr. Julian C. McPheeters, the Glide Foundation of San Francisco, California, designated a sum of money for a permanent lectureship in Asbury Theological Seminary. Lately the lectureship has been continued by a friend in memory of Mrs. Lizzie Glide. This provides each year for the services of some leader in the realm of Christian thought and life.

The George and Elisabeth Freitas Lectureship was established by Mrs. Elisabeth Freitas of Modesto, California, as a memorial to her husband, and as an expression of her interest in the training of a ministry on the highest level in spiritual attainment and practical achievement.

On January 26, 1960, the Board of Trustees of Asbury Theological Seminary established "The Julian C. McPheeters Missions Foundation" in honor of President McPheeters. The Board in May of the same year determined that all the interest from all funds given to this Foundation were to be used for the holding of an annual Missionary Conference. A goal of twenty thousand dollars was set for this Foundation.

The Martha R. Jones Lectureship was established in 1960. Martha R. Jones, Ph.D., an active member of The Methodist Church, who has devoted her entire lifetime to research in the field of nutrition, provided a trust fund at Asbury Theological Seminary in order to provide an annual lectureship in the field of nutrition. The purpose of this lectureship is to give to students-especially those preparing to be missionaries to under-developed areas of the world-a working knowledge of food values, and to teach by demonstration the relationship between soil, nutrition, and health.

The Minister's Conference

As is stated in the Seminary's catalogue for 1962-63, in keeping with its historic policy, Asbury Theological Seminary is earnestly endeavoring to make a positive spiritual and constructive theological contribution to the church by means of an annual Ministers' Conference. The underlying objective is best formulated in the statement of purpose:

> To emphasize the content of the Christian message and the deepening of the spiritual life.
> To face fearlessly the religious and theological problems of our day.

The Ministers' Conference really grew out of the Glide Lectureship. This series was begun in 1943 with Dr. E. Stanley Jones as the lecturer, and they have been continued annually with some outstanding Christian leader presenting the major addresses. The quality of these messages was of such a lofty order that President McPheeters believed they should be made available to a larger number of ministers in America. Therefore, in 1945 the Ministers' Conference was instituted under the joint sponsorship of Asbury College and Asbury Theological Seminary.

This has been one of the fastest growing parts of the Seminary's life. Through the years it has extended its influence among many states and to a variety of denominations. The expansion of the program and the quality of leadership has intensified a continuing interest among ministers and Christian workers throughout the states. The registration of the delegates for the Ministers' Conference held in January 1963, showed a total of 654, of which 532 were ministers and 122 were laymen. These came from 27 states and Guatemala and represented 23 denominations.

The Asbury Seminarian

The faculty of Asbury Theological Seminary have published from 1946 a semi-annual theological journal. This publication has maintained as its stated purpose the presentation of "the Wesleyan message in the life and thought of today." It includes in its pages articles by faculty and administrative officers of the Seminary, and submitted articles by others who share the theological heritage of the Seminary. This journal was carefully instituted and was accompanied by a clear expression of the purpose for which it was brought into being. President McPheeters asserted at the beginning that it would be a positive and cooperative instrument among the many theological journals that were already in existence. "It is our hope that we might be an added voice in reaching a constituency which will add to the sum total of those which are contending for the 'faith once delivered to the saints.'" *The Seminarian* has continued to share the generous support of the Student Body, and forms a living link between the institution and its alumni and friends.

The Master's Program in Theology Restored

Among those advances that were intended to strengthen the position and influence of the Seminary was the restoration of a Master of Theology program. With the addition of two new faculty members in September 1963, this master's degree was to be offered in two departments. The opportunities for studies leading toward the master's degree in other departments were to be made available as faculty additions made them possible.

Chapter 9
Accreditation—Lost and Recovered

The marked progress made by the Seminary toward accreditation undoubtedly began at the time of its separation from Asbury College. The college prior to 1939 had been seeking admittance into the Southern Association of Colleges, Universities, and Secondary Schools as an accredited member. At this time it was encouraged to expect such accreditation upon the fulfillment of two conditions: (1) to reach an endowment of one-half million dollars, and (2) to effect a complete separation from the Seminary. These requirements created many difficulties for both institutions. However, the process of separation was effectively begun in the fall of 1939. At the beginning of this academic year the Seminary first operated on a separate campus with its own faculty and curriculum. Procedures in the direction of complete independence were to continue for about three years. It was not until October of 1942 that the ultimate separation of the two Boards of Trustees was achieved. It is evident that during these years in which the two institutions were striving for independence that there was an increasing recognition of the necessity of more universal academic standing. During the earliest years of the Seminary such status was not as urgently demanded. While such an academically recognized position for

Asbury among the sister theological institutions of America was certainly highly desirable from the very beginning, the actual realization of this position was not definitely sought until about 1940, seventeen years from the time of its beginning.

With the ultimate objective of full accreditation in mind the administration and faculty began to indicate some of the conditions that needed to be fulfilled in order to achieve such academic recognition. In 1940, there were only four professors regularly engaged in full-time teaching. Two years later when this number had been satisfactorily increased the Seminary's application for accreditation was rejected, not because of too few faculty members, but rather because of insufficient endowment. Within a period of a few months following this first rejection by the American Association of Theological Schools the endowment was substantially increased and Asbury's application to the accrediting agency was renewed. This application, however, was not acted upon until February of 1944 when the Executive Secretary of the A.A.T.S., Dr. J. Gould Wickey, visited Asbury Seminary and made his report to the Association. Among Asburians, high hopes for the coveted prize followed the visit of Dr. Wickey, but at it's meeting in June 1944, the application was denied because of the limitation of library facilities.

The second official visit of Dr. Wickey to Asbury representing the American Association of Theological Schools was in the spring of 1946. The Secretary then expressed his very great pleasure at the marked improvement, which the Seminary had made since his visit in 1944. The one outstanding remaining weakness was the low level of professor's salaries. The recommendation that these be raised to a minimum of three thousand dollars was approved by the trustees of the Seminary, and on June 11, 1946, Asbury Theological Seminary was approved by this accrediting agency and thus was received into the membership of the American Association of Theological Schools. This was indeed one of the great days in the life of Asbury. At the age of twenty-three this institution had now taken its place among the older and honored theological institutions of higher learning in America. Undoubtedly this very important academic achievement became one of the contributing factors in giving rise to the sharp rise in student enrollment during the next three years. According to the registrar's files the increase was from 217 in 1946 to 349 in 1949, or a gain of 132 in three years. This is very likely the most meaningful advance in the number of students during the forty years of the Seminary's life.

This recognition of Asbury's advanced academic standing seemed to give greater impetus to her progress along many lines. The increase in material equipment, including several new major and minor buildings, brought its total assets to about one and a half million dollars. The strengthening of the faculty both quantitatively and qualitatively, the presence of a goodly number of representative students from several other nations, all became significant evidences of new life and vigor.

It may seem somewhat unusual that the young institution was relatively free of those growing pains that so often attend the years of such rapid growth. Yet this period of growing up was not to remain completely free of such disturbances.

During the school year of 1948-49 there arose upon the campus a concern about the theological position of one of Asbury's professors. The misgivings about the views of Professor Claude Thompson persisted unofficially until it became necessary for the administration through its Board of Trustees to act. The Board through its special committee on investigation concluded that Professor Thompson had "unnecessarily disturbed the campus by contending against a mechanical literalness which is not prevalent in Asbury Theological Seminary." Though the resignation was submitted immediately following this investigation it was not accepted by the Trustees, and Professor Thompson was retained with certain admonitions, especially that in the future he proceed with greater wisdom in his treatment of speculative questions.

The conflict in unofficial circles continued with increasing momentum during the weeks of the following year (1949-50), and the pressures for the resignation of Professor Thompson were multiplied. As late as May 1950, the Board of Trustees meeting in special session to review the Thompson case, by a vote of 13 to 1 confirmed his position as professor of doctrine. It is also important to observe that the Board clearly affirmed that,

> In whatever criticism of Professor Thompson this report implies, the committee calls in question neither the moral integrity nor the Christian character of Professor Thompson, both of which are readily acknowledged by his supporters and his critics.

However, when the Board met at the time of its regular session, May 27, 1950, a letter of resignation from Professor Thompson was presented by President McPheeters. This was then accepted, and although the case was thus officially closed, many theological differences continued to be expressed throughout the Asbury family.

The practical effect of the continuation of these divisive issues upon the campus of Asbury was of such a serious nature in the opinion of the American Association of Theological Schools that the Seminary suffered the loss of accreditation in December 1951. As President McPheeters has observed, it is significant that the same year that accreditation was revoked by the American Association of Theological Schools; accreditation was granted for the degree of Master of Religious Education by the American Association of Schools of Religious Education.

The loss of accreditation was a severe blow, but Asbury under the leadership of its president and Board of Trustees faced the situation with remarkable courage. The struggle was destined to be long and difficult, but every resource was brought into play; and though the process involved a period of nearly nine years all conditions were ultimately met and the effort of many was at last realized. The continued growth of the Seminary was clearly evident even during these years without accreditation. There was of course a marked decrease in enrollment at the time of the loss of accreditation, but the student body was never far below two hundred. Even with such a handicap the institution moved steadily forward, increasing its number of buildings, enlarging its endowment, expanding its faculty, and lifting its general morale.

In May 1955, the service of a counselor approved by the American Association of Theological Schools was employed. The recommendations made were carefully followed and a second request for reaccreditation was soon presented. This request was also refused. Beaten temporarily, but not broken or discouraged, a spirit of hopefulness prevailed throughout the Asbury administration, faculty, and student body. As President McPheeters has asserted, the coming of Dr. Frank Bateman Stanger in September 1959, as the Executive Vice President marked another significant advance in the life of the Seminary. Much of the ultimate achievement in the struggle for reaccreditation was the result of his wise leadership in academic administration. Dr. Stanger, with the commission on reaccreditation of the Board, kept in close contact with the Executive officers of the accrediting agency, and prepared very thoroughly for the visitation of the association's counselors to the Seminary, October 12-15, 1959.

The confidence of Dr. Stanger as Executive Vice President concerning the worthiness of Asbury to be accredited is expressed in a letter, which he addressed to Dr. Charles L. Taylor, Executive Director of the American Association of Theological Schools. Two paragraphs from that letter read:

> I have found at Asbury Theological Seminary a faculty consisting of individuals who I believe are academically qualified, spiritually concerned, and pedagogically effective. I have discovered a curriculum, which I believe, represents a sincere attempt to provide a balanced theological preparation for those who will serve in the Christian ministry. The curriculum is under the constant scrutiny of the faculty, and changes, such as the revaluation of the core curriculum and the introduction of courses of contemporary relevance, are effected whenever deemed wise. I would say that the academic morale of the Seminary is excellent.
>
> I am deeply impressed by the student body here at the Seminary. For the most part I have discovered young men and women characterized by a seriousness of purpose, a sense of Divine Call, a love of the truth, and a concern for the spiritual needs of the world. I have noted a deep desire on the part of the students to prepare themselves as fully as possible for the tasks to which they have been called.

Being encouraged by the evaluation of Asbury, which was made by this team of official visitors, once more an application for reaccreditation was presented in December 1959. In response to this request the American Association sent a team of official inspectors to the campus in April 1960. The report of these inspectors to the next regular meeting of the Association, which was held in Richmond, Virginia, was favorable; and on June 7, 1960, the report of the Accrediting Commission declared: "Accreditation is restored to Asbury Theological Seminary." This major achievement in the academic life of the Seminary brought a new day of opportunity for service such as it had never had before. In the spirit of great faith and optimism so characteristic of President McPheeters, he observed in commenting on this great success, "The struggles through which the Seminary has passed in its attainment of re-accreditation have made it a stronger institution than it could otherwise have been."

The very great significance of this achievement was likewise recognized by Dr. Stanger. In writing upon the subject in the September 1960, issue of the *Advance*, President Stanger affirmed with deep conviction

> The reality of the re-accreditation of Asbury Theological Seminary by the American Association of Theological Schools presents to the Seminary the greatest challenge in its history. An understanding of the full implications of this challenge will impel all those who truly love Asbury Theological Seminary to a new dedication of concern and prayer and contribution.

Chapter 10
Organizational Transition

The history of the office of the vice-president of Asbury Theological Seminary is varied. The several functions, which this person has been called upon to perform at various times, have prevented any real uniformity or consistency within this office. At times it has seemed that his major responsibility was to act locally in place of the president while the latter was away from the campus so much of the time. For instance, following the death of President Morrison in 1942, the Rev. Dr. Julian C. McPheeters served as acting president of the Seminary while still remaining as the pastor of Glide Memorial Methodist Church in California. This kind of administrative arrangement made the local work and leadership of the vice-president very urgent. Strangely enough, only during two of these six years (1942-48) in which President McPheeters remained in California, was the office of vice-president filled. The Rev. Dr. B. Joseph Martin served the Seminary in this capacity from 1946 to 1948.

However, in the years when this office was technically vacant, the responsibilities under President McPheeters were very faithfully and effectively performed by the Dean and the Business Manager. Matters of great academic concern including the wise and scholarly leadership of the faculty was accomplished by the untiring skill of Dean William D.

Turkington. In the realm of business and organization the life of the Seminary was well preserved and promoted by the good counsel and careful concern of Mr. William E. Savage. These were days of heroic service rendered by both these men when the fact of an absentee president often brought upon them duties that naturally would have been assumed by the vice-president.

Five men have served the Seminary as vice-president during its lifetime. The Rev. Dr. Louis R. Akers served from 1925 to 1932; the Rev. Mr. Robert H. Williams from 1932 to 1937; the Rev. Dr. Zachary T. Johnson from 1937 to 1940. The office remained vacant for six years (1940-1946), after which the Rev. Dr. B. Joseph Martin was elected in 1946 and served for two years. Again, upon the retirement of Dr. Martin in 1948, the office of vice-president was unoccupied. It was at this time that President McPheeters resigned from his pastoral ministry at the Glide Memorial Church and assumed his permanent residence on the campus of Asbury Seminary. No doubt the pressure of lack of finances at this time led the Seminary to conclude that the strength of a full-time resident president would make it possible for the institution to function successfully without a regular vice-president. This policy was continued throughout most of the fifties, but as had been assumed before, much of the work, which normally would have been assigned to the office of the vice-president, was accomplished by the Dean and Business Manager.

The rapid growth of the Seminary during the years of the fifth decade of this century so multiplied the responsibilities of the president's office that it was considered the part of wisdom to add to the administrative staff an executive vice-president. The president's duties were not only multiplied, but off-campus duties called him away much of the time. The cultivation of friends who were influenced to give generous support to Asbury became for him an important ministry. The editorship of *The Herald* called for wise and careful administration. This was not only a significant medium of truth for the Holiness Movement, but also, a timely instrument of cultivation working constantly in behalf of the Seminary. President McPheeters was likewise a preacher and evangelist in constant demand among the churches and camp meetings throughout the States. While these duties, other then the presidency, formed a supplement and support to the life of the institution, they required much of the president's time and energy to be used away from home.

Following the very enthusiastic recommendation of President McPheeters, the Board of Trustees elected the Rev. Dr. Frank Bateman Stanger to the office of Executive Vice-President in 1959. Dr. Stanger came to this office from a most successful ministry in the New Jersey Annual Conference. His last appointment there was as pastor of the large and influential congregation at Collingswood, New Jersey, where he had served with distinction for eight years. The work of Dr. Stanger was constituted primarily in the realm of academic concerns. As chairman of the faculty he set about to determine some clearly defined areas of responsibility and operation.

In his report to the Trustees, January 26, 1960, the Executive Vice-President presented several recommendations that would require constitutional changes. These emphasized the necessity of defining the duties and proper functioning of the major officers of administrative and academic leadership, such as, the President, Vice-President, Dean, Business Manager, Registrar, and Librarian. Also the divisional chairmen were chosen and appointed to the five major areas of theological education:

1) Applied Theology
2) Biblical Literature
3) Christian Education
4) Church History and Missions
5) Theology and Philosophy of Religion

These chairmen were to constitute two major committees involved in the administration of academic affairs: first, the committee of divisional chairmen, of which the Executive Vice-President is the chairman, was formed to act as an academic cabinet for the administration; and second, the curriculum committee, of which the Dean is the chairman and in charge of the entire instructional procedure of the Seminary. The regular faculty committees were also fully activated and the duties of each were clearly defined.

Further, the instructional ranks of the faculty were determined and their duties definitely indicated. The following categories were indicated: full professor, associate professor, assistant professor, and visiting professor.

Perhaps the greater transition came in the life of the Seminary, both from the point of view of general and academic administration, at the time of Dr. Stanger's election to the presidency upon the retirement of President McPheeters on May 28, 1962, Dr. Stanger became the third president of Asbury Theological Seminary. The great respect, the genuine appreciation, and the utmost confidence which the retiring president had in his successor is expressed in the following words:

> As I approached the age of retirement under the By-laws of the Seminary, my successor was made a matter of much prayer. One of the most significant administrative acts during a period of twenty years was the nomination of

Dr. Frank Bateman Stanger as the Executive Vice-President of the Seminary, with a view to his eventually becoming president. Dr. Stanger's record as the Executive Vice-President has demonstrated clearly that he was God's man to become the president of the Seminary upon my retirement. There is every indication that the progress and expansion of the Seminary for the next twenty years will be far greater than that which came during the twenty years of my administration.

In addition to and upon the basis of the elements of reorganization, which had taken place during the years immediately preceding 1962, more extensive readjustment was to follow. The office of Executive Vice-President was abolished as of May 28, 1962. At the same time two new offices were created, namely, an administrative assistant to the president and a Director of Stewardship. Further, it was fixed that the Director of the Expansion Program was to be related to the president's office.

Professional administrative assistance was obtained from the American City Bureau of Chicago, Illinois. The major purpose for the employment of these counseling services was to safeguard the administrative procedures during the period of reorganizational transition, and also to give guidance to the Expansion Program.

The Board of Trustees adopted a five-year Expansion Program for the Seminary in January 1961. The financial goals of this expansion totaled $3,700,000.00. One and a half million was designated for new buildings; one million for additional endowment to maintain new buildings; and one and one fifth million for endowment for academic expansion. Upon his retirement from the presidency, Dr. McPheeters was chosen as Director of the Expansion Program. In January of 1963 the Director reported that approximately one million dollars had been secured in cash and pledges during the first two years of the program.

The retirement of Dr. Julian C. McPheeters as the second president of Asbury Theological Seminary was appropriately and colorfully observed by a series of well-prepared occasions. This man of God and great spiritual leader of His people had served a well-loved institution with great fidelity and effectiveness during a period of twenty years when the traveling was exceedingly difficult, but when a goodly number of important victories were won. A grateful institution was therefore desirous of showing its sincere appreciation to one who had demonstrated such splendid consecration. This series of events was begun by a luncheon in honor of the retiring president, which was given by the Board of Trustees. This was followed by an all-Seminary Testimonial that was held in Estes Chapel and at which time the life and service of the honored guest were presented in rapid review. A high moment of this occasion was the establishing of the McPheeters Mission Foundation given to provide funds for the holding of an Annual Missionary Conference on the Asbury campus. The series was concluded with a Faculty and Staff dinner in honor of Dr. McPheeters at the Beaumont Inn, Harrodsburg, Kentucky.

The inauguration of President Stanger, October 11, 1962, was the first such official occasion in the history of the Seminary. Approximately a thousand attended this meaningful gathering on the campus in front of the Henry Clay Morrison Administration Building amid one of the largest and most widely represented assemblages ever to gather on the campus of this thirty-nine year old institution. Seventy-three delegates from various colleges, universities, and theological seminaries throughout the United States as well as delegates from denominational and interdenominational bodies were present.

In his inaugural address the President affirmed concerning the imperative of relevance in contemporary theological education: "A 'new man' in a 'new society' in this 'new age' demands that our theological seminaries train and send forth 'new ministers,' fully equipped to be relevant to serve effectively the needs of our day." He further declared:

> We hold firmly to the basic beliefs of historical Christianity. We believe in the full inspiration and absolute authority of the word of God. We affirm a Trinitarian view of God. In our confession of the atonement we declare that 'God was in Christ reconciling the world unto Himself.' With the Reformers who rediscovered the apostolic emphasis, we profess that justification is by faith alone. Suffice it to say that Asbury Theological Seminary rejoices in the Wesleyan Arminian emphasis upon the satisfying certainties of spiritual experience and the realizable ideals of Christian Holiness. Wesley's doctrine of the witness of the Spirit is a cherished truth. Just so, the Wesleyan doctrine of Christian Perfection, with both its personal realization and its social manifestations, is accepted as the *summum bonum* of spiritual experience.

Dr. Stanger concluded this emphasis by pointing out that, "We hold to a confessional position, not for the sake of being blind worshippers of 'the gods of tradition,' but because we are convinced of its religious validity and its spiritual vitality.

We have seen our theology at work in the lives of individuals, in the church, and in nations through the years."

The presiding officer at the inauguration was the Rev. Dr. C. I. Armstrong, chairman of the Board of Trustees. The Rev. Dr. Paul S. Rees, vice-president-at-large of World Vision, Inc. delivered the address in honor of the occasion. Bishop J. Waskom Pickett, retired Methodist missionary to India and native of Wilmore, read the charge to the new president. Dr. Armstrong, acting in official capacity, performed the act which officially bestowed upon Dr. Stanger all the privileges, benefits, and obligations of the president of Asbury Theological Seminary. Dr. C. Ralston Smith, a friend of Dr. Stanger since college days and now minister of the First Presbyterian Church, Oklahoma City, Oklahoma, offered the dedicatory prayer.

Others taking part in the ceremonies were: the Honorable Bert T. Combs, Governor of Kentucky; Dr. Z. T. Johnson, President of Asbury College; Dr. Charles L. Taylor, Executive Secretary of the American Association of Theological Schools; Dr. Allen W. Graves, President of the American Association of Schools of Religious Education; Dr. W. D. Turkington, Dean of the Seminary; and Dr. Julian C. McPheeters, President Emeritus and director of expansion at Asbury Seminary.

The inaugural luncheon for official delegates and friends was held at the Student Union Building on the campus of the University of Kentucky immediately following the conclusion of the inauguration ceremonies.

This highly formal inauguration of the third president of Asbury Theological Seminary was a day that was destined to be long remembered by members, friends, and associates of this institution. It was a most meaningful occasion for the Seminary academically, spiritually, and from the point of view of public relations. The church, educational institutions in America, and the theological world in general have no doubt become more aware of the status and function of Asbury than they were previous to this far-reaching affair. It has borne a lasting witness to the nature and purpose of this graduate theological school at home and abroad. The major ideas and doctrines of the founding fathers were reaffirmed. The reasonableness of and urgent need of such a theological and practical position were clearly indicated, and the enthusiastic response to such a presentation was exceedingly encouraging.

The effect of such a day of inspiration was likewise to be felt upon the home-life of the Seminary. In reviewing the significant achievements of the past and laying hold more firmly upon the necessities of the present there came a renewed unity of purpose among the administrators, faculty, staff, and students. A new sense of togetherness in a great cause commanded an increased measure of devotion and loyalty among all who participated. It was also a time of realistic optimism concerning the future of the Seminary. The humble expression of such confident hope and assurance was spoken by the retiring President McPheeters when he wrote "There is every indication that the progress and expansion of Asbury Seminary for the next twenty years will be far greater than that which came during the twenty years of my administration." Likewise a unity of aspiration and confidence was expressed by President Stanger in his report to the Trustees in January 1963, "We are participating in the rich heritage of the past. We rejoice in the rewarding advantages of the present. We resolve to seize the unprecedented opportunities of the future."

As the time of the retirement of Dean William D. Turkington approached, certain changes in administrative policy were contemplated. The constant increase and multiplication of responsibilities in the dean's office seemed to indicate the necessity of certain division of labors. In some measure as an experimental procedure President Stanger announced on April 10, 1963 the following plan for the expansion of the dean's office:

> Through the forty years of its history, Asbury Theological Seminary has been served by dedicated and faithful deans. We pause to pay respect to the memory of the late Deans Frank Paul Morris and Fred Halsey Larabee, and to salute the retiring dean, William D. Turkington. To be the inheritors of such a succession of worthy deans has inevitably resulted in a sobering sense of responsibility and stewardship in the selection of a new dean.
>
> In view of the administrative transition through which Asbury Theological Seminary is now passing, and after months of careful study and prayerful consideration, I have come to the conclusion that it is wise to create some kind of temporary administrative structure in the Dean's office. It has, likewise, seemed practical to work out a satisfactory division of labor among the many duties naturally falling within the area of the Dean's office.
>
> I am convinced that such a division of labor, within the limits of a temporary tenure of office, has decided practical advantages: (1) It will permit a satisfying experiment in discovering whether such a division of labor ought to be made permanent; (2) it will enable the members of the faculty chosen for these temporary assignments to discover any basis for a practical balance between academic and administrative

duties being carried on at the same time; (3) it will enable the President of the Seminary and the Faculty Committee of the Board of Trustees to continue a conscientious search for the most eminently qualified person, or persons, to fill such a position, or positions, before any administrative structure in relation to the Dean's office is made permanent.

In the light of the above reasoning, I have divided the labors of the Dean's office into the following four administrative areas:

1)   Acting Dean of the Faculty
2)   Acting Director of Admissions
3)   Acting Director of Graduate Studies
4)   Counselor of Students

The Acting Dean of the Faculty shall be in charge of all academic matters relating to the administration of all academic matters relating to the administration of the B. D. and M. R. E. programs. He shall serve as the Chairman of the Curriculum and Instruction Committee.

The Acting Director of Admissions shall be in charge of administrative work in reference to all admissions to the B. D. and M. R. E. programs. He shall serve as the Chairman of the Admissions Committee.

The Acting Director of Graduate Studies shall be the administrator of the newly established Master of Theology program. He shall be responsible for the setting up of the administrative and academic structure of the Master's program and shall supervise the continuing program. He shall serve as the Chairman of the Committee on Graduate Studies.

The Counselor of Students shall assume those duties that normally devolve upon a Dean of Men or a Dean of Students. He shall serve as the Chairman of the Vocational Guidance Committee.

I take this opportunity to announce officially the following appointments:

Acting Dean of the Faculty—
Dr. J. Harold Greenlee
Effective May 28, 1963

Acting Director of Admissions—
Dr. Howard F. Shipps
Effective April 10, 1963

Acting Director of Graduate Studies—
Dr. W. Curry Mavis
Effective April 10, 1963

It is understood by the Administration and each appointee that this is a temporary appointment, for a period not to exceed two years; that the appointment has been made in each case to meet an immediate interim administrative need; and that it has been made without precedent or prejudice in relation to future administrative succession when any or all of these temporary positions may be replaced or made permanent.

I extend my personal congratulations to Professors Greenlee, Shipps, and Mavis, and rejoice in the opportunity of serving with these colleagues in these new administrative relationships. I pledge to each one my cooperation and counsel and prayers.

(Signed) Frank Bateman Stanger

Chapter 11
In Retrospect and What
Prospect of Tomorrow

This has been a very brief and hasty review of the major events and achievements in the life of Asbury Theological Seminary during the first four decades of its life. As an institution it is still young and vigorous. It has also during more recent years of maturing been obtaining through valuable experience an increasing measure of wisdom, poise, and confidence. The years of difficulty, sometimes resulting in partial failure, as well as the years of achievement and success have contributed much to her store of knowledge and wisdom.

In retrospect Asbury looks back across the events and advances of forty years. One must be amazed as he meditates upon those things, which God has wrought through the instrumentality of this institution. Its founder could not have possibly dreamed of all the remarkable advances, which have come to pass in the good providence of God. The achievements of these years may be likened to those of the early days of American Methodism.

At the opening session of the General Conference in New York in 1812, William McKendree, the first native-born bishop of American Methodism, was directing the attention of the Conference to the marvelous things which God had wrought during the first twenty-eight years of its life. The Bishop said,—

> Upon examination, you will find that this work of the Lord is progressing in our lands. We had an increase of 40,000 members. At present we have 2,000 local preachers, and about 190,000 members, and these are widely scattered over seventeen states, besides the several territorial settlements and the Canadas.
>
> Thus situated it must be expected, in the present state of things, that the counsel and direction of your united wisdom will be necessary to preserve the harmony and peace of the body, as well as the cooperation of the traveling and local ministry, in carrying on the blessed work of reformation which the Lord has been pleased to effect through our instrumentality. To deserve the confidence of the local ministry and membership, as well as to retain confidence in ourselves and in each other, is undoubtedly our duty. And if we consider that those who are to confide in us are a collection from all classes and descriptions, and from all countries of which our nation is composed, scattered promiscuously over this vast continent- men who were originally of different educations, manners, habits, opinions, we shall see the difficulty as well as the importance of this part of our charge.

It is upon the basis of such outstanding success that McKendree made his telling appeal to the present. Likewise it may be appropriate that we hear these expressions of clear calling to devoted service in our day of great opportunity.

The Bishop continued further with his appeal,

> In order to enjoy the comforts of peace and union, we must "love one another." But this cannot abide where confidence does not exist, and purity of intention, manifested by proper actions, is the very foundation and support of confidence. Thus "united we stand" —each member is a support to the body, and the body supports each member, but if confidence fail, love will grow cold, peace will be broken, and "divided we fall." It therefore becomes this body, which by its example is to direct the course of thousands of ministers and tens of thousands of members, to pay strict attention to the simplicity of gospel manners, and to do everything as in the immediate presence of God.

As Bishop McKendree stood between two eras of Methodism, so Asbury stands at this fortieth anniversary. It reviews the past with appreciation and sincere gratitude. It faces the future with a real sense of reliance upon God and with a wholesome confidence that it shall be able to meet the demands of the future.

During these forty years from the time of its founding in 1923, Asbury Theological Seminary has achieved a place of high honor among her sister institutions throughout America. She is fully accredited by the American Association of Theological Schools and the American Association of Schools of Religious Education. In enrollment among accredited seminaries she ranks 20th. In percentage of growth among the top twenty accredited seminaries she ranks 4th. Among all accredited seminaries in rate of growth she ranks 15th. Her rate of growth since 1956 has been 21 percent.

Materially the Seminary is free from all indebtedness, having erected 27 buildings at a cost of $1,300,000. Its endowment is now $5,000,000 which makes the total assets $6,300,000. The life of any institution cannot be measured by its material possessions, but these may become a significant and tangible expression of its faith and life.

In addition to these material achievements, the Seminary has sent forth 1573 graduates. This is an average of 39+ each year. These graduates are serving God and the church through many types of ministry in 49 states, the District of Columbia, in 42 foreign countries, among 41 denominations, and under the direction of 20 mission boards.

The future calls for this greater Asbury to continue to send forth Spirit-filled, well-trained men of God into all the world. The answer to that call is now being formulated. Among the major objectives, which have been proclaimed by President Stanger, are: First, a real sense of community within the Asbury family. This calls for a thoroughgoing cooperation, which can only be achieved by the unity of the Spirit for which Jesus prayed in His high priestly prayer. This community of life and service must prevail among members of administration, faculty, staff, students, and friends in order that its normal effect may be realized in an abundance of fruit bearing within the kingdom of God.

Second, there must be an academic responsibility and maturity, which adequately justifies Asbury's position among the outstanding institutions of higher education throughout the world. The happy union of heart and mind, and the proper emphasis upon the combination of the spiritual and intellectual training must be preserved.

Third, the whole life of the institution must be preserved by a continuing spiritual vitality. Individually, collectively, and in unity we must be daily aware of and responsive to the Presence of God in our midst. Learning, administration, business, fellowship, service are all primarily dependent upon this.

In this kind of devotion, commitment, and unity of the Spirit Asbury faces the future unafraid.

Supplement A:
Articles of Incorporation

Know all men by these presents, That the undersigned, namely: H. C. Morrison, Louisville, Kentucky, F. H. Larabee, Wilmore, Kentucky, F. P. Morris, Wilmore, Kentucky, J. C. McPheeters, San Francisco, California, W. H. Butler, Atlanta, Georgia, Virgil Moore, Lexington, Kentucky, Bettie Morrison, Louisville, Kentucky, J. H. Pritchard, O'Bannon's, Kentucky, W. W. Holland, Cincinnati, Ohio and J. M. Brafford, Moundsville, West Virginia, have associated themselves together for the purpose of forming a corporation under the laws of the State of Kentucky, and in accordance with Article VIII, of Chapter 32, of Kentucky Statutes Editions of 1922 and 1930.

(1) The name of the corporation is, **Asbury Theological Seminary.**

(2) The corporation has the right to sue and be sued, contract and be contracted with, have and use a common seal, and alter the same, at pleasure.

(3) The principal place of business and office of the corporation shall be in the City of Wilmore, County of Jessamine, and State of Kentucky.

(4) The business, nature, and purpose, proposed to be transacted, promoted and carried on, and the object of the corporation are:

> (A) To have, to hold, retain, possess, all real, personal, or mixed property that may hereafter be given, granted, devised, conveyed, alienated and presented to said institution of learning, as may be necessary to carry on or promote the objects of the corporation:

> (B) To have power to alienate, sell, or convey or transfer or mortgage or pledge or dispose of, all or any part of the said real, personal or mixed property; at its pleasure;

> (C) Provided, however, if any real, personal, or mixed property has been received as a gift or devised for some special purpose and if so received it shall be used and applied only for such purposes.

> (D) To maintain the corporation as a Theological Seminary for the promotion of Theological Education. It will be the object of this Seminary to prepare and send forth a well-trained, sanctified, Spirit-filled, Evangelistic Ministry. This Seminary will emphasize in its teaching the divine inspiration and infallibility of the Holy Scripture, the Virgin Birth, Godhead, Vicarious Sufferings, and bodily resurrection of our Lord Jesus Christ. The instruction of this Seminary will fully recognize the fallen estate of mankind, the necessity of individual regeneration, the witness of the Spirit, the remains of the carnal nature, and entire sanctification as a definite second work of grace subsequent to regeneration. The instruction in this Seminary will conform fully to the Wesleyan interpretation of the Scripture. The instructors in this institution will guard

with jealous care against any sort of teaching in sympathy with modern liberalism.

(E) No person shall be elected to the Board of Trustees or to an official position, in this corporation, nor shall any person be employed as an instructor or assistant instructor, in its corps of teachers who is not in full sympathy with the Wesleyan interpretation of the Scriptures on Entire Sanctification, and who does not in humble faith trust in Christ for full deliverance from all sin.

(F) This corporation having been organized as a religious and educational one, any departure from or evasion of the objects and purposes stated, in subhead D and E, of head IV, of these articles of incorporation, will forfeit all and every right of the corporation to all and any gifts, grants, devices, conveyances, or presents, that may have been theretofore made to the corporation, by gift, grant, devise, deed or present, where provided for in writing and the donors, givers, or bestowers, their successors and real and personal representatives and heirs will have the right, power and authority to take steps to cause any and all gifts, grants, devises, whether real or personal or mixed property to revert to the donors or givers or their successors.

(G) It is the full purpose of the incorporation of this institution, and it must be the full purpose of the Trustees, Professors, and Students, of the corporation, by the use of all proper means to spread Scriptural Holiness over all these lands.

(5) This corporation being formed for religious and educational purposes has no capital stock. There is no private pecuniary

profit to be derived by any of the incorporators or organizers of the corporation.

(6) The said corporation shall commence business and the purposes for which it was organized as soon as permission is received therefore, from the Secretary of State, of the State of Kentucky, and shall continue for ninety nine (99) years from the date thereof.

(7) The affairs of this corporation shall be conducted by the incorporators until the first Tuesday of June 1932. On the first Tuesday in June, 1932, the said incorporators shall elect fifteen persons to serve as Trustees of the corporation and of the fifteen Trustees it shall be determined by drawing that the terms of three Trustees will expire on the first Tuesday of June A.D. 1933, A.D. 1934, A.D. 1935, A.D. 1936, A.D. 1937, respectively, it being the intention that the term of three Trustees will expire on the first Tuesday of June in each and every year. On the first Tuesday in June 1933, and every year thereafter, on the first Tuesday in June the Board of Trustees will elect three Trustees for a term of five years. All trustees are eligible for re-election for all successive terms. In the event a vacancy for any cause occurs in the Board the remaining Trustees shall elect his successor to hold the office until the next regular meeting of the Board of Trustees, and on that date the Board of trustees shall elect a Trustee to fill out the unexpired term. But, if the term expires on that date there will be no election to fill the vacancy, as there will be no vacancy to fill. All Trustees shall hold office respectively until their successors are elected and qualified.

All elections for Trustees shall be by ballot and shall be held in the State of Kentucky.

(8) The Board of Trustees may by its by-laws, change the annual meeting date, of the Board of Trustees.

(9) In the event the first Tuesday in June is a legal Holiday the annual meeting provided for thereon shall be held on the first day thereafter not a legal Holiday.

(10) The officers of the corporation shall be elected annually on the first Tuesday in June, and shall consist of a President, Vice-President, Secretary, and Treasurer; all of these officers shall hold office for a term of one year and until their successors are elected and qualified. In the event the first Tuesday in June is a legal Holiday, the annual meeting provided for herein shall be held on the first day thereafter not a legal Holiday. The President of the corporation shall be President of the Seminary and *ipso facto* a member of the Board of Trustees and Chairman of the Board of Trustees. The President of the corporation shall select all Teachers, Assistant Teachers, Professors, Assistant Professors, Tutors, and Employees of the corporation, provided, however, any and all such selections made by the said President shall be subject to the approval or ratification of the Board of Trustees.

(11) The President or any seven (7) members of the Board of Trustees, exclusive of the President, at any time may call a special meeting of the Board of Trustees.

(12) The Board of Trustees may at any special or general or annual meeting remove any Officer, Teacher, Assistant Teacher, Professor, Assistant Professor, Tutor, or discharge any Employee of the said institution.

(13) The said corporation may adopt by-laws for its government but the said by-laws must not be contrary to the laws of the United States or of the State of Kentucky, or this Charter.

(14) This corporation shall not incur indebtedness in excess of over the sum of Five Thousand ($5,000.00) Dollars.[1]

(15) This corporation shall have the power to confer on graduates proper degrees in theology. It may also confer Theological Degrees, on any person that its Board of Trustees may deem to be entitled thereto.

(16) The private property of the Contributors, donors, incorporators, and members of the Board of Trustees, and the officers of the corporation shall be exempt from the corporate debts of the institution.

(17) If by any means Asbury Theological Seminary should in any way be absorbed, united or placed under the control of any other institution, then all donors, givers or bestowers to said Asbury Theological Seminary, their successors and real and personal representatives and heirs shall have the right, power and authority to take steps to cause any and all gifts, grants, and devises, whether of real or personal or mixed property to revert to the donors or givers, or their successors.

In Testimony Whereof, Witness the signatures of the incorporators this 4th day of June, A.D. 1931.[2]

H. C. Morrison   F. H. Larabee

F. P. Morris   J. C. McPheeters

W. H. Butler   Virgil Moore

Bettie Morrison   J. H. Pritchard

W. W. Holland   J. M. Brafford

Notes

---

[1] Raised to $50,000 on October 18, 1946; to $250,000 on May 30, 1947; to $500,000 on December 1-4, 1948.

[2] The names of the signators were identical with the names listed in the beginning of these Articles.

Supplement B:
The Full Time Faculty

The members of the faculty who have served God through the medium of Asbury Theological Seminary are numerous. Some have stayed with the institution a relatively short time; others have given the larger part of their whole life. The list represents persons of a considerable variety of abilities and many gifts of the Spirit. The sons and daughters of Asbury recognize in all these worthy saints and scholars those whom God has chosen for such a holy task. The following list proposes to include all who have participated in this sacred ministry of theological education.

The original listed ended in the 1960's. With this new edition of the book, the list has been updated thanks to Kenneth Cain Kinghorn's book *The Story of Asbury Theological Seminary*[1]. The Provost Office has provided the faculty information from 2010 till 2012[2].

Faculty Appointments in the 1920's

1) Daisy Dean Gray (1923-1924; 1927-1938)
2) Edmund J. Guest (1923-1924)
3) Walter E. Harrison (1923-1930)
4) Fred Halsey Larabee (1923-1949)
5) Frank Paul Morris (1923-1948)

6)   Henry Clay Morrison (1923-1942)
7)   Wilder Robert Reynolds (1923-1938; 1946-1953)
8)   George W. Ridout (1923-1932)
9)   Lewis Robison Akers (1926-1932)
10) William David Akers (1926-1934)
11) Claude Lee Hawkins (1926-1931)
12) John Wesley Hughes (1926-1927; 1929-1932)
13) Wilbur Olin Allen (1927-1933)
14) William David Turkington (1927-1940; 1943-1963)
15) Samuel Arthur Maxwell (1928-1934)
16) William Lincoln Nofcier (1928-1934)

Faculty Appointments in the 1930's

17) Harold Marcus Hillard (1931-1935)
18) John Martin Maxey (1931-1933)
19) Philip A. Clapp (1931-1933)
20) Mary Elizabeth Corley (1932-1934)
21) Harry Emerson Rosenberger (1932-1934)
22) Hildreth M. Cross (1934-1945)
23) Mildred L. Stanhope (1936-1938)
24) Zachary Taylor Johnson (1937-1940)
25) Ada B. Carroll (1937-1938; 1943-1962)
26) Ruth Little (1937-1938)
27) Gaile J. Morris (1937-1948)
28) Peter Wiseman (1937-1940)
29) Mary Chambelain (1939-1940)

Faculty Appointments in the 1940's

30) Allan Robert Moore (1940-1943)
31) John Haywood Paul (1941-1946)

32) R. F. Ockerman (1941-1948; 1950-1951)
33) Kenneth Plank Wesche (1941-1946)
34) Julian Claudius McPheeters (1942-1962)
35) George Wilcher (1942-1943)
36) Harold Barnes Kuhn (1944-1982)
37) J. Harold Greenlee (1944-1965)
38) B Joseph Martin (1944-1948)
39) Adolphus Gilliam (1945-1946)
40) Annie Kartozian (1945-1946)
41) Lena Barbara Nofcier (1945-1949)
42) George Allan Turner (1945-1979)
43) Ollie Mae Williams (1945-1949)
44) Clarence V. Hunter (1946-1948)
45) Majel Michel (1946-1947)
46) Russell R. Patton (1946-1947)
47) James D. Robertson (1946-1975)
48) W. Curry Mavis (1947-1974)
49) Rodney William Long (1947-1952)
50) C. Elvan Olmstead (1947-1948)
51) Claude H. Thompson (1947-1950)
52) Paul F. Abel (1948-1949)
53) Harold C. Mason (1948-1962)
54) Robert P. Shuler, Jr. (1948-1951)
55) John S. Tremaine (1948-1951; 1966-1982)
56) Jack Howard Goodwin (1949-1952)
57) Susan A. Schultz (1949-1978)
58) Ruth A. Warnock (1949-1962)

Faculty Appointments in the 1950's

59) Earle E. Barrett (1950-1952)
60) William M. Arnett (1951-1989)
61) Ophel B. Crockett (1951-1952)

62) Ralph D. Lowell (1951-1952)
63) Ruth E. Nussey (1951-1953)
64) Harold Paul Sloan (1951-1952)
65) James Herbert Whitworth (1951-1953)
66) Willard Roy Hallman (1952-1968)
67) Delbert R. Rose (1952-1975)
68) Percival A. Wesche (1952-1954)
69) George Herbert Livingston (1953-1986)
70) Howard F. Shipps (1953-1973)
71) Robert A Coleman (1955-1983)
72) Hammond W. Porter (1955-1958)
73) Verna M. Culver (1956-1966)
74) Lloyd H. Franke (1956-1957)
75) Robert L. Anderson (1957-1962)
76) Wilber T. Dayton (1957-1971)
77) John T. Seamands (1957-1960; 1962-1987)
78) Elisabeth Batten Edwards (1958-1968)
79) Nyle DeFresne Hallman (1958-1960)
80) Roy Hallman (1958-1960)
81) Martha R. Jones (1958-1960)
82) Frank J. Kline (1958-1959)
83) Grace B. Ely (1959-1960)
84) Roy Hallman (1959-1960)
85) Frank Bateman Stanger (1959-1986)

Faculty Appointments in the 1960's

86) Ralph Loren Lewis (1961-1990)
87) Paul Hudson Wood (1961-1970)
88) John J. Shepard (1961-1966)
89) Onva K. Boshears, Jr. (1962-1970)
90) J. Waskom Pickett (1962-1963)
91) William Coker (1963-1965; 1968-1970)
92) Alice M Kann (1963-1965)

93) Dennis Kinlaw (1963-1968; 1982-1983)
94) Thomas A. Carruth (1964-1982)
95) Maurice Culver (1964-1966)
96) Ivan C. Howard (1964-1968)
97) Charles David Stokes (1964-1965)
98) David E. Edwards (1965-1966)
99) John E. Hartley (1965-1966)
100) Gilbert M. James (1965-1980)
101) Kenneth Cain Kinghorn (1965-2003)
102) K. C. Matthew (1965-1966)
103) Wayne McCown (1965-1966)
104) Marilyn Walker Morrison (1965-1971)
105) Ronald D. Worden (1965-1966)
106) Donald E. Demaray (1966-2000)
107) Robert W. Lyon (1966-1997)
108) Leslie Marston (1966)
109) L. Ernest Otter (1966-1967)
110) Robert A. Traina (1966-1988)
111) Harry Richard Weeks (1966-1968)
112) Charles Whiston (1966)
113) Wayne Woodward (1966-1967)
114) Robert J. Gailer (1967-1969)
115) Harvey J. S. Blaney (1967-1968)
116) Herbert W. Byrne (1967-1989)
117) William C. Cessna (1967-1979)
118) Ray N. Cooley, Jr. (1967-1982)
119) C. Barron Buchanan (1968-1985)
120) Fred D. Layman (1968-1998)
121) Gene Lemcio (1968-1969; 1972-1973)
122) Carl Eugene Pavey (1968-1969)
123) Donald Dayton (1969-1972)
124) Glenn A. McNeil (1969-1970)
125) Eric Mount (1969-1970)
126) Frank Shirbroun (1969-1971)

Faculty Appointments in the 1970's

127) Saphir P. Athyal (1970-1971)
128) William Faupel (1970-1975; 1977-2004)
129) Charles D. Killian (1970-2004)
130) John N. Oswalt (1970-1982; 1989-1999; 2009-)
131) Joseph Wang (1970-2004)
132) Loal C. Ames (1971-1974)
133) Anthony Casurella, Jr. (1971-1973)
134) Kenneth E. Gooden (1971-1977)
135) Donald M. Joy (1971-1998)
136) John A. Seery (1971-2004)
137) Ivan L. Zabilka (1971)
138) Avid L. McIlvaine (1972-1974)
139) William H. McKain, Jr. (1972-1978)
140) Jerry L. Mercer (1972-1999)
141) Stephen R. Sebert (1973-1977)
142) Stanley R. Beck (1974-1979; 1988-1989)
143) Philip Roughton (1974)
144) Melvin E. Dieter (1975-1990)
145) James A. Hewett (1975-1976)
146) Dennis McCardle (1975-1989)
147) Steven Robert Miller (1975-1976)
148) Dale Eugene Pickard (1975-1976)
149) Ivan Timm (1975-1981)
150) Charles Turkington (1975-1980)
151) Frederick C. Van Tatenhove (1975-2002)
152) Louis Caister (1976-1983)
153) Ronald W. Crown (1976-1978; 1987-1988)
154) Kenneth A. Hudacsko (1976-1979)
155) R. Wade Paschal (1976-1978; 1991-1993)
156) David L. Thompson (1976-1983; 1986-2013)
157) Laurence W. Wood (1976-)

158) Michael Boody (1977-1984)
159) Donald Boyd (1977-2000)
160) Allan Coppedge (1977-2011)
161) Wayne E. Goodwin (1977-1986)
162) Harold Burgess (1978-1989)
163) O. Ray Fitzgerald (1978-1985)
164) Matthew R. Goldner (1978-1980)
165) C. Reginald Johnson (1978-)
166) Michael R. Keller (1978-1981)
167) David W. Kendall (1978-1981)
168) V. James Mannoia (1978-1994)
169) Frederick W. Schmidt, Jr. (1978-1980)
170) Ralph Wesley (1978-1981)
171) Arthur S. Brown (1979-1989)
172) M. Robert Mulholland, Jr. (1979-2009)
173) Albert W. Sweazy (1979-1983)

Faculty Appointments in the 1980's

174) Ralph J. Coleson (1980-1982)
175) Joseph R. Dongell (1980-1983; 1989-)
176) Steven J. Harper (1980-1993; 1997-2012)
177) Jonathan A. Hunt (1980-1982)
178) Samuel T. Kamaleson (1980-1981)
179) John W. Landon (1980-2000)
180) Linda Rickman (1980-1987)
181) Kenneth A. Boyd (1981-2011)
182) Donald Butterworth (1981-1987)
183) Donald Conrad (1981)
184) Charles Kingsley (1981)
185) John Vayhinger (1981-1984)
186) Clayton N. Crow (1982-1958)
187) Larry E. Freels (1982-1989)

188) David L. McKenna (1982-1994)
189) Frank C. Norris (1982-1986)
190) Charles Sims (1982-1986)
191) Della Blackburn (1983-1984)
192) Melvin R. Bowdan (1983-1989)
193) Eugene E. Carpenter (1983-1989)
194) Ronald Crandall (1983-2008)
195) David Gyertson (1983-1984)
196) George G. Hunter, III (1983-2011)
197) Leon Hynson (1983-1985)
198) Donald Keyon (1983-1984)
199) John Kilner (1983-1992)
200) Malcolm McVeigh (1983-1985)
201) Keith H. Reeves (1983-1984)
202) Randy R. Richardson (1983-1986)
203) David A. Seamands (1983-1992)
204) Stephen A. Seamands (1983-)
205) Howard A. Snyder (1983-1985; 1996-2006)
206) Mathias Zahniser (1983-2000)
207) David R. Bauer (1984-)
208) David D. Bundy (1984-1989)
209) Mary Fisher (1984-2004)
210) Thelma M. Goold (1984-1988)
211) Margaret Therkelson (1984-1987)
212) Darrell Whiteman (1984-2004)
213) Albin Whitworth (1984-2004)
214) Bradford L. Fipps (1985-1986)
215) Joan Lyon (1985-1989)
216) J. Steven O'Malley (1985-)
217) Philip A. Amerson (1986-1989)
218) Beatrice H. Holtz (1986-1988)
219) Kenneth Andrew McElhanon (1986-1990)
220) Helen D. Musick (1986-1989; 2000)
221) Rory P. Skelly (1986-1988)
222) Benjamin S. Baker (1987-1989)

223) Richard Boone (1987-1989)
224) Virginia Bowles (1987-2002)
225) A. B. Broderson (1987-1989)
226) William C. Goold (1987-)
227) Phyllis Hail (1987-1989)
228) Lawson G. Stone (1987-)
229) Catherine Stonehouse (1987-2011)
230) Jerry L. Walls (1987-2008)
231) Felix W. Sung (1988-1989)
232) Ole Borgen (1989-1992)
233) Christine Pohl (1989-)

Faculty Appointments in the 1990's

234) Leslie A. Andrews (1990-2013)
235) Anthony J. Headley (1990-)
236) Everett N. Hunt, Jr. (1991-1996)
237) John Walters (1991-1999)
238) Burrell Dinkins (1992-2006)
239) Ellsworth J. Kalas (1993-2011)
240) Maxie Dunnam (1994-2004)
241) Eunice L. Irwin (1994-)
242) Bill T. Arnold (1995-)
243) Kenneth J. Collins (1995-)
244) Dale Galloway (1995-2004)
245) Virginia Todd Holeman (1995-)
246) Barbara Holsinger (1995-2006)
247) James R. Thobaben (1995-)
248) Robert G. Tuttle, Jr. (1995-2010)
249) Ben Witherington, III (1995-)
250) Joel B. Green (1997-2006)
251) Joy Moore (1997-2007)
252) Paul Chilcote (1998-2005)

253) Brian Dodd (1998-1999)
254) Christ A. Kiesling (1998-)
255) Brent Strawn (1998-2001)
256) Howe O. (Tom) Thomas, Jr. (1998-2003)
257) Richard L. Gray (1999-)
258) Charles E. Gutenson (1999-2009)
259) William James Patrick (1999-)
260) Thomas F. Tumblin (1999-)

Faculty Appointments in the 2000's

261) Hugo Magallanes (2000-2007)
262) Tapiwa Mucherera (2000-)
263) Terry C. Muck (2000-2011)
264) Stuart L. Palmer (2000-2005)
265) Ruth Anne Reese (2000-)
266) Sandra Richter (2000-2008)
267) Brian Russell (2000-)
268) Lester Ruth (2000-2011)
269) Daryl L. Smith (2000-)
270) Steve Moore (2001-2006)
271) Garwood Anderson (2002-2007)
272) Meesaeng Lee Choi (2002-)
273) Beverly Johnson-Miller (2002-)
274) Michael Pasquarello, III (2002-)
275) Zaida Maldonado Pérez (2002-)
276) Michael A. Rynkiewich (2002-2010)
277) Russell West (2002-)
278) Tory Baucum (2003-2007)
279) James K. Hampton (2003-)
280) Jeffrey Greenway (2004-2006)
281) Stephen L. Martyn (2004-)
282) Stacy R. Minger (2004-)
283) Thomas Buchan (2006-2012)

284) Randy Jessen (2006-2009)
285) Kevin Kinghorn (2006-)
286) Arthur McPhee (2006-)
287) Lalsangkima Pachuau (2006-)
288) José Javier Sierra (2006-)
289) Stephen P. Stratton (2006-)
290) Steven J. Ybarrola (2006-)
291) Brian Edgar (2007-)
292) Fredrick Long (2007-)
293) Ellen Marmon (2007-)
294) John A. Cook (2008-)
295) Anne K. Gatobu (2008-)
296) John Hong (2008-2011)
297) Michael Matlock (2008-)
298) James C. Miller (2008-)
299) Joseph B. Okello (2008-)
300) Timothy C. Tennent (2009-)

Faculty Appointments in the 2010's

301) Deb Colwill (2011)
302) Steve Offutt (2011-)
303) Gregg Okesson (2011-)
304) Angel Santiago-Vendrell (2011-)
305) Bryan Sims (2011-)
306) Jeffrey Frymire (2012-)
307) Doug Matthews (2012-)

Notes

---

[1] Kinghorn, Kenneth Cain. *The Story of Asbury Theological Seminary.* Emmeth Press: Lexington, Kentucky, 2010. pp. 465-472. Dr. Kinghorn's book has the names arranged in alphabetical order.

[2] First Fruits would like to thank the Provost office and Peg Keeley for taking the time to help update list of faculty members.